REVELATION AND THEOLOGY
VOLUME II

Theological Soundings •

REVELATION and THEOLOGY

VOLUME II

by E. Schillebeeckx, O.P.

translated by N. D. Smith

SHEED AND WARD:NEW YORK

75577

© Sheed and Ward, Inc., 1968

Originally published as parts 1 and 2 of *Openbaring en Theologie* (Theologische Peilingen, I), Uitgeverij H. Nelissen, Bilthoven (1964). This translation is based on the second revised edition of 1966.

Library of Congress Catalog Card Number 67-21907

Nihil Obstat
 Leo J. Steady, Ph.D., S.T.D.
 Censor Librorum

Imprimatur
 ✠ Robert F. Joyce
 Bishop of Burlington
 January 3, 1968

The Nihil Obstat and Imprimatur are official declarations that a book or pamphlet is considered to be free of doctrinal or moral error. No implication is contained therein that those who have granted the Nihil Obstat or Imprimatur agree with the contents, opinions or statements expressed.

Manufactured in the United States of America

Contents

Contents   vii

Abbreviations

BT	St. Thomas Aquinas, *In Boethium de Trinitate*
BThom	*Bulletin Thomiste*, La Saulchoir 1924ff.
CIC	*Codex Iuris Canonici*, Rome 1918
Conc.	*Concilium*, London 1965ff.
DN	St. Thomas Aquinas, *De Divinis Nominibus*
DR	H. Denzinger, *Enchiridion Symbolorum, Definitionum et Declarationum de Rebus Fidei et Morum*, ed. Karl Rahner, Freiburg 1953²⁹
DS	H. Denzinger, *Enchiridion Symbolorum*, ed. Adolf Schönmetzer, Freiburg 1963³²
ER	St. Thomas Aquinas, *In Epistulam ad Romanos*
Greg.	*Gregorianum*, Rome 1920ff.
KA	*Katholiek Archief*
NRT	*Nouvelle Revue Théologique*, Louvain 1925ff.
PL	*Patrologiae Cursus completus, Series Latina*, ed. J. P. Migne, Paris 1844ff.
Potent.	St. Thomas Aquinas, *De Potentia*
Quodl.	St. Thomas Aquinas, *Quodlibeta Disputata*
RNP	*Revue Néoscolastique de Philosophie*, Louvain 1894ff.
RSPT	*Revue de Sciences Philosophiques et Théologiques*, Paris 1907ff.
RSR	*Recherches de Science Religieuse*, Paris 1910ff.
RT	*Revue Thomiste*, Brussels 1893ff.
SCG	St. Thomas Aquinas, *Summa Contra Gentiles*
1, 2, 3, 4 Sent.	St. Thomas Aquinas, *In Quattuor Sententiarum P. Lombardi Libros*, I, II, III, IV

ST	St. Thomas Aquinas, *Summa Theologiae*
TP	*Tidschrift voor Philosophie*, Louvain 1929ff.
TT	*Tidschrift voor Theologie*
Verit.	St. Thomas Aquinas, *De Veritate*
ZKT	*Zeitschrift für Katholische Theologie*, Innsbruck 1877ff.

REVELATION AND THEOLOGY

VOLUME II

I

THE VALUE OF OUR SPEECH ABOUT GOD AND OF OUR CONCEPTS OF FAITH

1

1 The Concept of "Truth"

The problems concerning the concepts *truth* and *reality* which demand consideration by the Second Vatican Council in various forms may be discussed under three headings: (1) *truth* and the possession of truth; (2) the conceptual character of our knowledge, and Modernism; and (3) the problem of the reinterpretation of dogma.

TRUTH IN ITSELF AND TRUTH AS A POSSESSION

1. Our present thinking is characterized by a critical attitude towards the rationalism of previous centuries. Long before even the emergence of existentialism, thought which, in the Hellenistic climate of Western civilisation, was to a very great extent orientated towards the consideration of abstract and universal and unchangeable truths had changed course and was moving in a direction whose motto was *vers le concret,* back to the concrete, shifting reality. It was from this background of modern thought that both existentialism and phenomenology emerged; but from it also emerged a great variety of attempts on the part of neo-Thomist thinkers to reassess human thought as a faculty of truth whereby reality could be meaningfully encountered, according to the way in which this reality discloses itself to the activity of human thought which both extracts and gives meaning. Conceptual, rational thought is contrasted with lived experience, *l'ex-*

5

périence vécue. Present-day thought is clearly reacting on the one hand against idealism, according to which human thought itself creatively produces its contents and therefore truth, and on the other hand against the "representational realism" of scholasticism, which regards the content of our concepts as an exact reflection of reality without any reference to a human act which confers meaning. This reaction against these two trends of thought clearly moves in two directions. On the one hand, it tends in the direction of phenomenology, one of the basic affirmations of which is that the world is essentially a "world-for-me." In other words, reality has no independent, absolute meaning, but many different significations in relation to man, and these significations vary according to the standpoint from which man approaches or deals with reality. Indeed, according to many modern phenomenologists, the objective signification of a reality can be found only in the meaning that this reality has in relation to man. On the other hand, there is also the trend of thought followed by certain Catholic philosophers (especially de Petter and Strasser) who claim that, implicit in the relative meanings given by man, there is an absolute meaning in reality. This meaning is, in their view, independent of human thought and acts, in its absolute value, as the norm for all meanings given by man. This second movement attempts to gear what is true in phenomenological thought to what may be called the insights of the *philosophia perennis,* but this perennial philosophy is consequently placed in a perspective which is entirely different from that in which it was seen in scholastic thought.

The notion of truth has thus become much more "supple" in modern thought—so supple, in fact, that it has in many cases moved in the direction of complete relativism. The modern insight that the essence of man is inseparable from his historicity has, of its very nature, resulted in a more flexible view of truth than the traditional one, according to which man is seen in terms of a human nature that has been permanently defined once and for all time and is incapable of being inwardly conditioned by concrete, changing circumstances. In the modern view, insofar as it accepts an absolute reality at all, reality (as truth) is seen as the never-wholly-to-be-deciphered background of all our human interpretations. The ontological basis, as the mysterious source of a still-hidden fullness of meaning, remains the same and does not change, but the human interpretation of this basis, and thus man's possession of truth, grows and evolves. This is, however, drawn in one definite direction by this implicit ontological significance, so that truth is always approached more and more concretely, even though it is never completely apprehended.

If we disregard the relativist views, according to which no absolute truth exists (a view which is, of course, implicitly atheistic), we are nonetheless forced, by experience itself, to affirm—against the background of the absolute truth that determines our thought as a norm—the imperfection and the evolving and relative nature of our possession of truth, and consequently the fact that our earlier insights are capable of inexhaustible amplification. It is the fundamental orientation to the absolute implicit in all our knowledge which gives continuity to our human and constantly changing consciousness. From a finite, limited, constantly changing, and historical standpoint, we have a view of absolute truth, although we never have this in our power. In this sense, we cannot say that truth changes. We cannot therefore say that what was true before is now untrue, for even our affirmation of truth does not change or become obsolete. The standpoints from which we approach truth, however, are changing continuously and our knowledge is thus always growing inwardly. The whole of our human knowledge is, in its orientation towards the absolute, also coloured by these standpoints. It is, however, at the same time apparent from the fact that we are aware of the existence of these perspectives from which we view absolute truth that we rise above relativism. We do not possess a *conscience survolante*, an awareness that is able to transcend all relative standpoints and thus survey objective reality. Yet this is still the view held in many scholastic circles with regard to truth. The consequence of this is that differences of view are frequently confused with the relativist tendencies that are in fact present in modern thought.

It is at the same time clear, from this "perspectivism" of our knowledge (which is orientated towards absolute reality and also regulated by it), that man's insight into truth will never lead to complete unanimity. Our maintaining an open and receptive attitude in our affirmation of the truth towards what is true in the views of others is, anyway, a condition for the attainment of the highest possible degree of unanimity.

2. We have also achieved in recent years a more modulated insight into the multi-dimensional nature of the human world of truth.[1]

Thus there is, for example, the truth of the everyday, practical world, the truth of modern positive science, the truth to which philosophy aspires, and finally the truth which we attain and love in religious faith.[2]

Thus the truth of the positive sciences is confined to the world of phenomena. These sciences are therefore concerned only with the verifiable aspects of reality. As a result, these sciences do not cover the whole of reality and therefore

[1] See A. Dondeyne, *Geloof en Wereld*, Antwerp and Bilthoven 1962, 147 ff.
[2] Dondeyne, 148.

cannot claim to replace metaphysical and religious truths. But neither should someone who is convinced of his affirmations of metaphysical and religious truths simply play these off against the partial values of the positive sciences. The first attitude would lead to dogmatic positivism and scientism, and the second to a religious dogmatism that denies different levels of truth. In the problem of truth, we have therefore to take into account the multi-dimensional character of truth, which cannot be reduced to one single type of truth. This view too has not yet generally penetrated into every Catholic circle.

THE VALUE OF OUR CONCEPTS; MODERNISM

The conceptual, and therefore the abstract, element of thought plays an unmistakable part in the distinction between "truth-in-itself" and truth "as a human possession." The question of how our concepts of faith are related to truth occupies a central position in the present critical stage of development in theological thought.

The Scholastic Tradition as Opposed to Modernism

In the scholastic tradition, especially after Scotus, the abstract character of our concepts was regarded as the reason for our being able to apply them also to transcendent, divine realities.[3] The essence of this tendency is to be found in the affirmation that our concepts are really capable, not only of

[3] M. Pénido's *Le rôle de l'analogie en théologie dogmatique*, Paris 1931, is characteristic of this tendency and forms its classic expression. For a detailed treatment of our non-conceptual knowledge the reader is referred to the Appendix: "The Non-Conceptual Intellectual Dimension of Our Knowledge of God according to Aquinas."

reaching out for the reality of God, but also of grasping God conceptually. The same conceptual content could therefore be applied, in a proportionally analogical manner, both to the creature and to God. This view is still held even today in many scholastic circles.

In modern scholasticism, however, there has been a great deal of controversy about this centuries-old view, which has been held to be fundamentally conceptualistic. Among those who are opposed to this view are Sertillanges, Balthasar, L. de Raeymaker, and, in Holland, P. Kreling, who has further-more come to the conclusion that it is not Thomistic. According to Aquinas, we have no concepts of God, but only creaturely concepts, which we do not, however, attribute or assign to God, but via which we reach out for God without actually grasping him conceptually.

An early radical reaction against this conceptualism came from Modernism, which demanded that more attention should be given to the inward, subjective, non-conceptual aspect of the act of faith—that is, to religious experience or the aspect of non-conceptual knowledge that is, in this view, the real core of the faith of revelation.

According to Modernism as it was synthesised by G. Tyr-rell,[4] revelation was an act of God, with whom the believer came into mystical contact. This contact had no representa-tional aspects—revelation was not, in the Modernist view, a communication of truths. This wordless and non-conceptual contact with the God of revelation was certainly spontan-eously expressed and made explicit in a kind of prophetic knowledge, the elements of which were derived from the contemporary civilisation of the prophet who received the revelation, but even this first expression was no longer guaranteed by divine testimony. Theology could, in the

---

[4] Especially in his book, *Through Scylla and Charybdis*, London 1907.

Modernist view, only provide an interpretation of this prophetic content, and this theological interpretation was itself
entirely dependent on the contemporary level of civilisation.

According to Modernism, religious experience, in which
revelation was really accomplished, was a permanently unchangeable primordial phenomenon, occurring both within
the Church of Christ and outside it. The type or norm of
this experience was, however, the experience of the apostles
in their direct contact with Christ. The conceptual aspect
of faith simply surrounded this experience as a shield. In
this way, the concepts of faith were seen as a kind of conceptual reminiscence of the religious experience of the
apostles. For us they at the same time offered, as it were, an
opportunity of evocation, which would permit us to arouse
in ourselves an experience that was analogous to the experience of the apostles. This so-called tradition of the content
of revelation was, in the Modernist view, made possible by
the sense of God fundamentally possessed by every human
being. The believer recognised in the Church's external
preaching what he experienced inwardly. There was, however, according to the Modernists, no faith without this
personal aspect of experience. In their view, then, revelation
did not come from outside but was spoken into the soul by
the Spirit of God, into that "fine point" of the human spirit
which was receptive and listening to God. The Church's external presentation of the truths of faith was only an occasion
for the experience of faith.

This, then, is the basic conception of Modernism, which
is rather more subtle than some manuals suggest. It is clear
that Modernism gave a certain value to the tradition that
we find in Scripture and in the authentic teaching of the
Church.[5] But it will also be clear that for Modernism the

5 See Tyrrell, 307.

concepts or expressions of faith do not make us grasp reality
—they are simply symbolic expressions determined by existing social and historical conditions and therefore replaceable, expressions which from outside protected the real
mystery that is grasped non-conceptually in the central experience of faith, and at the same time to some extent
evoked it.

Tyrrell regarded his view as a middle course between extreme liberalism, which denied the continuity and the unchangeable character of dogma (maintaining that, although
the object of the doctrines of faith always remained the
same, doctrine itself underwent radical changes in the
course of history), and what he called "scholastic formalism,"
which regarded closed and unrepeatable revelation as a
theology in embryo from which the dogmas were dialec-
tically deduced under the pressure of contemporary neces-
sities.[6] Seeking a passage between this Scylla and that
Charybdis, Tyrrell affirmed that revelation was really unchangeable (it evolved neither formally nor materially), but
that all conceptual explicitation was radically changeable.
The two aspects of the act of faith—the aspect of experience
and the conceptual aspect—were therefore, according to
Tyrrell, completely separate. The conceptual aspect was
simply an extrinsic, symbolic, and pragmatic protection for
the real core of faith (the so-called revelation in time con-
sisting in this conceptual aspect).

Modernism, then, did indeed draw upon a fundamental
patristic and scholastic affirmation, thus formulated by Aquinas: "faith comes in principle by infusion"; but Aquinas'
equally essential complementary statement: "but in respect
of its content it comes by listening and hearing,"[7] was de-

---

[6] See Tyrrell, 116 ff.

[7] 4 *Sent.* d. 4, q. 2, sol. 3, ad 1: "fides principaliter est ex infusione,
sed quantum ad determinationem suam est ex auditu."

nied, or at least interpreted in a weakened, unorthodox sense. Modernism was an attempt to grasp the core of the act of faith, but it failed at the same time to appreciate the integral essence of this act—only the aspect of inner illumination was accepted and, dissociated from the expressions of faith (the *determinatio fidei*), this was inevitably bound to result in unorthodoxy.

Nonetheless, the Modernists did discover a real problem —that of the distinction between truth in itself and truth as a spiritual possession of man.[8]

The Discussion Leading up to Humani Generis

The "New Theology." The problem that Modernism was unable to solve—that is, the problem of the relationship between experience and concept—has continued to be a theological issue until today.

After many honest attempts had been made to find an answer to this problem, it was eventually taken up again by Bouillard.[9] This author made a distinction, in the conceptual theological knowledge of faith, between the aspect of judgment (*affirmation*), which he regarded as unchangeable, and the aspect of representation (*représentation*), which he regarded as evolving and replaceable. The constant basic affirmation was, in Bouillard's view, always contained in the continuously changing aspects of representation. Bouillard explained this by the fact that, in the evolution of one concept, all our concepts develop at the same time, but in such a way that the same original relationships continue to exist between these evolved concepts.

8 See A. Loisy, *Autour d'un petit livre,* Paris 1903, 190-92.
9 H. Bouillard, *Conversion et Grace chez saint Thomas d'Aquin,* Paris 1944, 211-24.

An unchangeable truth could therefore be affirmed in and through changeable concepts. It should, however, be noted here that Bouillard was not referring directly to the dogmatic concepts of faith (these pertained to the aspect of judgment), but only to those concepts of faith that were elaborated in theology (and which consequently pertained to the aspect of representation). This fact emerged from the controversy that arose over Bouillard's publication of his views. It should also be noted that the changeable and the unchangeable aspects were not placed side by side but were to be found within each other—in other words, that the conceptual framework did not contain the judgment of faith itself, but that the reality referred to through these concepts "remains one and the same."[10]

The reaction against Bouillard's thesis, and especially that of Labourdette and M. Nicolas, was partly based on a misunderstanding of what Bouillard was in fact saying. These theologians attacked the distinction that Bouillard had made between the aspect of judgment and that of representation, seeing in it a latent agnosticism with regard to the content of faith, in view of the fact that the absolute element of the affirmation was, according to Bouillard, only attained in and through the non-absolute element of the aspects of representation. They laid stress on the fact that the God who revealed himself in human language himself guarantees the relation between the concepts of faith and the reality of salvation, and is thus himself the guarantee of the truth of the concepts of faith. Theology was, in their view, the attempt at a more precise, reflective understanding of the reality in the concepts of faith. They even went so far as to maintain that theological terminology, despite its greater flexibility, aims at unchangeability, and that

10 H. Bouillard, "Notions conciliaires et analogie de la vérité," RSR 35 (1948), 255.

the dogmatic formulation was definitive even as a formulation.

In his reaction both against Bouillard and against Bouillard's opponents, Sträter said:

The formulation of dogma always has a limited value in that it is never an adequate expression of the concept the Church wishes to express in it, and in that this concept itself does not explicitly reflect the reality in its totality. The same formulation, however, has an absolute value in that the reality itself is grasped in the concept expressed in it and in that the formulation expresses some of the reality itself.[11]

Sträter thus merely transferred the problem to the sphere of the human awareness of Christ, who communicated the reality of salvation to us in a human manner in his revelation. His views about this are valuable, but they do not contribute to the solution of the problem of experience and concept. Insofar as Sträter did provide some solution to this problem, he would seem to follow Maritain and give a certain intuitive value to the conceptual as such.[12]

The reaction to the encyclical. Pope Pius XII defended the validity of our conceptual knowledge of God and of faith in the encyclical *Humani Generis,* which was written in reaction to the claim that our religious concepts have a purely pragmatic or symbolic meaning. This claim had not in fact been made by the theologians of the so-called new school (and in this context especially by Bouillard, whose thesis I have just discussed). But these writers had, after all, once more taken up the problem that had been left unsolved after the Modernist crisis, and had discussed this in terms which

---

11 C. Sträter, "De waarde der dogmatische formulering," *Jaarboek 1949 Werkgen. Kath. Theol. Nederl.,* Hilversum 1950, 194.
12 For this, see especially the discussion in Sträter, 198-201.

appeared to deviate markedly from the traditional scholastic view. What is more, their terseness, which often resulted in some lack of balance, had given the impression that they were giving way to a certain relativism. Reacting against this relativizing of our concepts of faith, the encyclical also affirmed that these concepts are adequately true. This does not, of course, mean that the encyclical was asserting that our concepts of faith adequately—that is, exhaustively—embraced the mystery of salvation. But, if this is taken as a starting-point, the concepts of faith remain adequately true —inadequately true concepts would, in the terminology of the encyclical, mean that these concepts did not grasp reality itself and consequently had no value for objective knowledge. But they have real objective value and this is unchangeably true, with the result that earlier definitions of faith can never become untrue later, even though these concepts may still be, as the encyclical added, refined, perfected and given new shades of meaning.

The tendency to go back to the sources, to return to the concepts of the Bible and the Fathers, was approved by the encyclical only if this attitude was not prompted by a depreciation of later conceptual formulations. The view that different, and mutually contradictory, systems together reflect the truth in a better and more adequate manner than one definite coherent system was also condemned by the encyclical.

What the encyclical was, however, basically intent throughout on stigmatising was relativism in dogma, in whatever form it appeared.

The Relationship between Experience and Concept in Modern Catholic Theology

As we have already seen, the representational conceptualism of scholasticism subsequent to Scotus, according to which

conceptual contents were directly applicable both to worldly
and to supramundane realities, led to an impasse in modern
neo-scholasticism. More fundamental attempts—more fundamental than, for example, the rather passing comments made
by Bouillard on the affirmation of truth and its presentation
already referred to—to solve the problem of the conceptual
nature of our knowledge have been made in recent years.
These have followed two different directions. On the one
hand, there has been the direction taken by Blondel and
explicitated in Thomist perspective by Maréchal (whose
work resulted in a school, among whose members I would
include, for example, Karl Rahner). On the other hand,
there is the direction taken by de Petter (who has been
followed in the theological field by the present writer).

The school of Maréchal: the dynamism of the spirit.
Confronted with Kant's criticism of speculative knowledge,
and under the influence, at the same time, of M. Blondel,
who regarded all human knowledge as supported by affective experience, J. Maréchal, S. J.,[13] seeing the impasse into
which scholastic conceptualism had got itself (for which
Modernism had been unable to find a satisfactory alterna-
tive) proceeded to deny that conceptual knowledge as such,
in and of itself, could reach reality. We cannot, therefore,
reach God with our human concepts, because their representational content is creaturely and hence is not applicable
to God. If we say God is good, then the representational
content of this goodness is inevitably a creaturely goodness.
How, then, can we call God good? From what does this
affirmation derive its validity, in spite of the creaturely—
and thus relative—character of its conceptual content? If
there is to be any truth in the affirmation "God is good,"

13 *Le point de départ de la métaphysique,* Louvain and Paris 1927[2],
Cahier I, 207 ff. See also "Le dynamisme intellectuel dans la connaissance
objective," *RNP* (1927), 137–165; and *Mélanges J. Maréchal,* Brussels and
Paris 1950, pt. 1.

an implicit confrontation must take place somewhere between creaturely goodness and the reality of God.

Maréchal provided a solution to this problem by basing the reality and validity of our knowledge of God not on these concepts in themselves, but on a non-intellectual, dynamic element—the dynamism of the human spirit towards the infinite. The conceptual contents are taken up in this dynamism of the spirit, and so this conceptual content is transcended and projected towards God. Our knowledge of God is, therefore, according to Maréchal, a projective act by means of which I reach out beyond the concept in the direction of God, thanks to the dynamic impulse of the spirit which animates the concept. Man is thus able to reach towards God via the conceptual content—towards God as the aim of the human capacity to know.[14]

What is unsatisfactory about Maréchal's solution is that it does not explain the distinctive meaning of every conceptual content; that the reality and validity of knowledge is based on an extra-intellectual element; and, finally, that while it does establish that human knowledge cannot remain stationary at anything finite, but must always be continuing to search and to explore other territories, it does not establish that man, in his knowledge, really attains a positive and infinitive end, God himself.

The school of de Petter: the "non-conceptual" dimension of knowledge. The school of de Petter is in accord with that of Maréchal in affirming that concepts as such cannot reach reality or truth, and therefore that they can do so only as elements of a greater whole. In addition, this trend of thought also affirms that a non-conceptual aspect is the basis of the validity of our conceptual knowledge. Maréchal did not, however, situate this non-conceptual aspect formally

[14] See Appendix: "The Non-Conceptual Intellectual Dimension in Our Knowledge of God according to Aquinas."

in a real intellectual element, but in an extra-intellectual element—that is, in the dynamism of the human spirit. De Petter and his followers, on the other hand, speak of a non-conceptual dimension of knowledge itself, and thus of an "objective dynamism"—that is, of an objective dynamic element in the contents themselves of our knowledge, which themselves refer to the infinite.

According to de Petter, the concept is

> . . . a limited expression of an awareness of reality that is in itself unexpressed, implicit, and pre-conceptual.[15]

This pre-conceptual awareness of reality is in itself not open to appropriate expression. Our concepts refer to this non-conceptual awareness essentially as to something that they aim to express, but to which they can only give inadequate and limited expression. It is therefore not an extra-intellectual dimension—the dynamism of the human spirit—that enables us to reach reality in our concepts, but a non-conceptual consciousness through which we become aware of the inadequacy of our concepts, and thus transcend our conceptual knowledge and approach reality, although in a manner that is no longer open to expression. According to this view, the concept, or the "conceived," has the value of a definite *reference* to the reality, which is, however, not grasped or possessed by it. By virtue of the inexpressible and non-conceptual consciousness which is implied in our explicit or conceptual knowledge, or in which this conceptual knowledge is included, the concept indicates the objective direction in which reality is to be found, and—what is more—indicates a *definite* direction—the direction which is inwardly pointed out by the abstract conceptual content.

15 See D. de Petter, *Begrip en werkelijkheid*, Hilversum 1964, esp. 25–136 and 168–173.

Therefore, although concepts are insufficient and even do not reach reality in themselves—that is, seen in their exclusive abstract character[16]—they have a certainly inadequate but nonetheless real truth and validity as included in the non-conceptual consciousness, because they—and they alone —impart a direction and meaning to the transcending beyond the concepts to reality. Experience and conceptual thought thus together constitute our single knowledge of reality.

I have shown, in a historical study of Aquinas,[17] that he had already defended, although not in a fully elaborated manner, the proposition that we cannot apply our concepts as such to God, as though one and the same concept (goodness, for example) might analogously but equally apply both to the creature and to God, but that the conceptual content of goodness is only the perspective in which we must situate God's goodness, without knowing how this content really also applies to God. Our knowledge therefore only comes into contact with God in conscious unknowing (the wholly Other). We know that God is good, although the conceptual content of this goodness is only a creaturely goodness and the divine mode of this goodness therefore escapes us. The typical intellectual value of our conceptual knowledge of God is therefore situated in a projective act in which we reach out towards God via the conceptual contents. In this, we cannot grasp God conceptually, although we do know that he is present in the objective and definite direction that is indicated by the contents of the concept.[18] In this way, the agnosticism that is inherent in the purely sym-

16 This is because what an abstract concept makes *known* is concretely, and therefore differently, realised in the concrete reality.

17 See the Appendix: "The Non-Conceptual Intellectual Dimension in Our Knowledge of God according to Aquinas."

18 See Volume I of this work, chapter 5: "What Is Theology?" pp. 87 ff.

bolic value of conceptualism according to Modernism (E. Le Roy) is overcome, and the older, Thomistic affirmation according to which the highest human knowledge is to be found in conscious unknowing (*theologia negativa*) is re-asserted.

This applies even more to our supernatural knowledge of faith. If our concepts are, in the case of our natural knowl-edge of God, naturally open to the transcendent, then our natural concepts are, in the case of the concepts of faith, made open by positive revelation to the expression of super-natural truths. The God who revealed himself in human form has given a new dimension to human contents of knowledge—a new objective perspective which these con-tents do not in themselves have for our human intellect as such, but which they only derive from revelation and thus from the non-conceptual aspect of our act of faith. This natural intellectual content, which is included in the super-natural act of faith, directs our spirit by virtue of revelation (and thus by virtue of the non-conceptual element in the act of faith) objectively to God's intimate life, which is not attainable by purely human knowledge. Thus, the father-hood and sonship of God, for example, are really an exten-sion of the reality, father and son, of our human experience, but we cannot grasp conceptually the manner in which this fatherhood and sonship is realised in God. In this, our con-cepts of faith are not purely symbols that are interchange-able with other symbols (as the Modernists believed), nor are they a purely pragmatic knowledge in the sense that we must behave towards God as a son behaves towards his father. We do not in fact apply the purely conceptual rep-resentational content of *father* and *son* to God, but we can, by extending that and no other conceptual content (that is, father and son), really reach God. Consequently, God is in himself Father and Son, although in such a way that we cannot form any real conception of this divine fatherhood and sonship.[19] Thus mystery and objective intelligibility are intimately connected with each other.

This view provides us, in my opinion, with the true perspective within which we can affirm both the absolute character of the truth of faith and the high degree of relativity and thus of growth in our reflection about faith. And all this is contained within the one human consciousness—this is not to be reduced exclusively to conceptual knowledge.

The Radical Accentuation of the Problem by Bultmann's "Demythologisation"

A recent attempt to go to the root of this problem has been made by the Protestant scholar R. Bultmann with his well-known theory of demythologisation (*Entmythologisierung*).[20] The scope of this view extends beyond our problem, but its radical attitude does at the same time provide a solution to the problem of the relationship between experience and concept. Bultmann made a distinction between scientific objectivising thought and personal existential thought. In this context, the difference between what is said (*das Gesagte*) and what is intended (*das Gemeinte*) is important. That is to say, there is a distinction between the manner of presenting an affirmation and its real intention or meaning, just as there is an existentialist distinction between the mode of being of material things (*das Vorhandene* or *das Dingliche*)

[19] See Volume I of the present work, chapter 5, "What Is Theology?", the section on the basis of the possibility of a speculative theology, pp. 119 ff.

[20] For a useful account and critique of Bultmann's views, and a select bibliography of the very considerable literature on this subject, see Joseph Bourke, "The Historical Jesus and the Kerygmatic Christ," *Conc.* I, 2 (1966), 16–26.

and the distinctive mode of existence of man (*die Existenz*). In other words, the existential is not susceptible to objectification. Thus God and the mystery of salvation can never be presented as objective. I cannot speak about God, therefore, except insofar as *he* speaks to me here and now in my existence. We can therefore only speak about God in existential categories. Dogmatic definitions, on the other hand, are of the objective order of material things (*das Dingliche*): they are consequently, according to Bultmann's theory, unintelligible and without content.

THE SO-CALLED "REINTERPRETATION OF DOGMA"

The word *dogma* had various meanings in the past—it meant doctrine, opinion, edict, and so on. In Hellenistic Judaism it was also used to mean "the divine edict," that is, the Mosaic law. But even in the patristic period, and especially from the fourth century onwards, it was applied expressly to the teaching of the Christian faith, especially in contrast to the teaching of Christian morals. It first acquired its now classic meaning, however, at the time of the Renaissance—every truth directly revealed, either explicitly or implicitly, by God. This truth must therefore be contained in Scripture or in unwritten tradition, and must moreover be proposed as divine revelation, to be explicitly confessed in faith by the extraordinary or the ordinary universal teaching authority of the Church. The First Vatican Council called these truths "divine and Catholic faith."[21] Only those truths of faith clearly possessing a dogmatic character were, however, called dogmas in canon law,[22] and it was moreover not always clear whether the *ordinary* universal teaching

[21] DS 3011 (= DR 1792).
[22] *CIC* 1323, para. 3.

authority of the Church aimed to propose a doctrine precisely as a revealed truth. For these reasons, it gradually came about that an even stricter, narrower meaning was given to dogma. In this stricter sense, only a truth revealed by God and as such solemnly defined by the Church's *extraordinary* teaching authority was called a dogma. Actually, however, this distinction is arbitrary. The very fact that a revealed truth is proposed by the Church's teaching authority makes it a dogma. Dogmas are therefore the Church's authentic expressions of a reality of revelation.

The Church's expressions, however, conceal a double relationship—that towards the contemporary situation in the Church, and that towards the original faith of the primitive Church made present in the experience of faith. In other words, in dogma the original apostolic experience of faith is heard at a particular time and in a particular situation in the Church. This living context does not distort the original faith, but allows it to be heard in a pure way precisely at this particular time. *Dogma* is therefore always an expression by the Church of the whole Church's experience of faith as this is made present again and again from the apostles' faith and throughout the history of the Church. A dogma is thus a new formulation, relating to a particular situation, of the mystery of salvation experienced in the Church— the experience of faith itself in a particular phase of ecclesiastical expression. In this sense, the special formulation, as the expression of the mystery of faith, *belongs with* the object of faith,[23] if the reservation is made that consent in faith to the dogma does not have the formulation itself as its end, but—via the dogma—the reality of the God of revelation.[24] Since the saving value of faith is based on its value as reality or truth, the dogmatic formulation itself, as the

23 Aquinas, *ST* II–II, q. 1, a. 2; *Verit.* q. 14, a. 8, ad 5.
24 *ST* II–II, q. 1, a. 2, ad 2.

Church's actualised experience of faith, also has, in principle, a religious significance.

This religious value of dogma was made even more explicit in the scholastic definition of dogma, that is, in the teaching of the article of faith (the *articulus fidei*). Aquinas especially regarded the dogmas as the central truths of faith which directly concerned the religious salvation of men and in relation to which all the other subordinate truths of faith were arranged.[25] In his view, the dogmas were the central truths of Christianity. The difference between the medieval and the modern concept of dogma is therefore that for Aquinas the dogmatic character of a truth of faith was clear from the inner structure of the content of faith, whereas modern theologians base this dogmatic character on the Church's definition of a revealed truth. The two insights are therefore complementary.

If we now look at the relationship of dogma to the mystery of salvation itself, it will be clear that, in the dogma, the mystery of faith is expressed in human concepts that can never be sufficient to convey the whole mystery. The dogma reflects the reality for salvation of the content of revelation from a particular point of view of the Church, and therefore insofar as this reality which is known by us in faith is conceptually and figuratively expressed in concepts and ideas of faith.

What is meant, therefore, by a dogmatic definition is the affirmation in faith of a saving reality together with the entire representational structure. The strictly conceptual aspect of this structure is its sharply defined intellectual aspect, which is, however, at the same time a part of the wider background of a historically conditioned world of ideas. A subtle distinction has therefore to be made in the definition

25 *ST* II–II, q. 1, a. 6.

of any dogma between the real essence of the dogmatic affirmation—that is, what is necessary if we are to move towards the inexpressible content of faith in a true and authentic way—and the secondary aspects relating to the form in which the definition is couched. In making this distinction, however, we must bear in mind that no pure formulation, independent of human concepts, of the apostolic truth can ever be reached, but that this absolute truth can always only be seen in conceptual terms, with the result that the absolute and relative aspects of dogma can never be placed exactly side by side. Our movement towards the reality of salvation by means of dogma has to be satisfied with imperfect concepts. It is therefore impossible to separate the experience and the conceptual framework of faith. What is more, as the absolute core of faith, towards which we move in these concepts, is also expressed in and mixed with the kind of presuppositions that are already present in men's minds at the time, there are, in certain dogmatic formulations, representational aspects which are entirely conditioned by the prevailing historical situation and which can consequently by changed at a later period. Human experience, precise scientific data, and similar factors can help to purify the way in which dogma is presented. An example of this is the idea of Christ's ascension, the representation of which was formerly connected in the minds of the faithful with the ancient view of the world. What was only a mode of expression in the implicit intention of the definition was automatically conceived in the minds of the faithful as forming part of what was itself expressed or affirmed.

The dogmatic meaning continues unchanged whenever these older forms of expression are changed. The study of the growth of various dogmas reveals quite clearly that developments have in fact taken place by progressive explicitation and that these developments have given rise to

new definitions, that have—within the limits of the unchangeable unity of dogmatic meaning—been more explicit
than earlier insights. There have also been developments in
the history of dogma that have taken place, so to speak, by
a process of breaking off. This does not mean that part of
the original meaning may have ceased to apply, but that
the original meaning has eventually been freed from the
confused terminology of the historical situation in which
it had developed. It is furthermore quite clear that, before
this purification, the Catholic faith was not explicitly conscious of the fact that the (obsolete) view of man and the
world in which these dogmas were thought out was not
really important to what the dogmas were actually stating.
In the initial period, when no distinction was made, the
Church automatically spoke—as did all the faithful—as if
the mode of expression formed part of the essence of dogma,
without meaning this expressly, however, or even being able
to mean it. It is only when new human experience or new
positive data explicitly raise the question of the distinction
between the content of faith and its form that it is possible
to see clearly whether the so-called form of expression is
simply a mode of representing the dogma or whether it
forms an essential part of the dogmatic content.

The reinterpretation of dogma can therefore have both
an orthodox and an unorthodox significance. If the aim of
this reinterpretation is to purify our insights into faith of
their earlier, and now obsolete, forms of expression (for
example, to dissociate the ascension of Christ from the Pto-
lemaic cosmology) it will have an orthodox Catholic meaning, and what was originally intended through the use of
this older form of representation will remain inviolably true.
A truth can also be expressed in forms which are in themselves incorrect, but which are able, in a given social situation, very suggestively to formulate the envisaged truth.

Whenever anyone says, "I love you, my angel," although he does not mean that the woman he loves is really an angel, what he says does suggest a deep reality. In different cultural situations, however, such expressions may be quite meaningless.

The reinterpretation of dogma may also mean not only that the fringe of ideas representing the conceptual structure of the dogma in its historical setting is cut off, but also that this conceptual structure—insofar as this truly, if not exhaustively, expresses the reality of salvation—is itself presented in a more subtly shaded manner. This may occur, for example, when existential ideas are used instead of physical concepts. It is precisely because our knowledge is always gained from approaching the reality of salvation from a definite standpoint or perspective that this truly constant insight can be integrated into a higher insight or augmented by complementary insights when it is viewed from different standpoints. What has once been declared a dogma can never be revoked, but it can certainly be integrated into newer insights in which its life really continues, even though this may be in a different perspective. In this connection, however, it is important to bear in mind that the new insights are not extrinsic to the older definitions, added to them as appendices, but that the truths seen earlier have been thought out again in the new insights. Finally, it should be quite clear that the reinterpretation of dogma will have an unorthodox significance if the view is accepted that this reinterpretation is possible and necessary because our concepts have a merely symbolic and pragmatic value.

These views may be said to be more or less generally accepted throughout the theological world of Western Europe. They have not, however, been accepted by a group of scholastic theologians who continue to regard human knowledge in rigidly conceptualistic terms, and who confuse the unchangeable character of truth with a representational view of human concepts. The representatives of this movement are obviously still (unjustifiably) afraid that, when all is said and done, the other movement does make concessions to relativism. In fact, all that this new movement seeks to do is to stress the way in which human—and therefore limited—knowledge can be directed towards the absolute truth—in other words, it emphasises the sense in which our knowledge is not relative, in spite of its constitutional limitations. What we are in fact witnessing here is the confrontation between what are, so to speak, two distinct spiritual worlds within the one Catholic faith.[26] The one tendency can readily adopt, at least in practice, the attitude that our human concepts are capable of containing the whole of reality and that we especially who are believers have a monopoly on truth. But the other tendency, when it is misapprehended or presented in an oversimplified form, can in fact court a hidden relativism.

[26] See my collections of articles: *Vatican II: the Struggle of Minds*, Dublin 1963; and *Vatican II: the Real Achievement*, London and New York 1967.

2 The Non-Conceptual Intellectual Element in the Act of Faith: A Reaction

Since the appearance, from 1910 onwards, of P. Rousselot's articles about the act of faith[1] and his book, *L'intellectualisme de saint Thomas*,[2] there has been a steady flow of books and articles about the "light of faith" and about the *instinctus fidei* or the "divine impulse which prompts and invites us to believe."[3] The experiential aspect of the act of faith,

[1] "Les yeux de la foi," *RSR* 1 (1910), 241–259, 444–475; "Remarques sur l'histoire de la notion de foi naturelle," *RSR* 4 (1913), 1–36.

[2] Paris 1926². Eng. trans., *The Intellectualism of St. Thomas*, London and New York, 1935.

[3] From the copious literature on this subject, I would mention the following books and articles: E. Dhanis, "Le problème de l'acte de foi," *NRT* 68 (1946), 26–43; "Révélation explicite," *Greg.* 34 (1953), 187–237; J. H. Walgrave, *Geloofwaardigheid en Apologetica* (Theologica. Voordrachten Vlaams Werkgenootschap voor Theologie), Ghent 1953, 16–24; J. de Wolf, *La justification de la foi chez saint Thomas et le père Rousselot*, Brussels and Paris, 1946; M. D. Chenu, *La psychologie de la foi dans la théologie du XIIIe siècle*, Paris and Ottawa, 1932; *Contribution à l'histoire du traité de la foi* (Mélanges thomistes), Kain 1923, 123–141; R. Aubert, *Le problème de l'acte de foi*, Louvain 1958³; F. Jansen, "La psychologie de la foi dans la théologie du XIIIe siècle," *NRT* 61 (1934), 604–615; L. Cornelissen, *Geloof zonder prediking*, Roermond 1946; I. Trethowan, *Certainty, Philosophical and Theological*, Westminster 1948; *The Basis of Belief*, London and New York, 1961; A. Stolz, *Glaubensgnade und Glaubenslicht nach Thomas von Aquin* (Stud. Anselmiana, n. 1), Rome 1933; B. Douroux,

which had disappeared in post-Tridentine speculation about the act of faith, has once again been accorded its proper place by these writers. Neglect of the "mystical aspect of faith" in the Fathers and the scholastic authors of the high Middle Ages had led to the act of faith being regarded more or less as a conclusion drawn from successful reasoning. A. Gardeil and R. Garrigou-Lagrange were the first to react against this impoverished theology of faith—partly as a result of the Modernist crisis in the Church—but even stronger reactions were evoked by historical studies of the light of faith in Thomas, Albert[4] and Bonaventure,[5] by the new movements in philosophy and by contemporary interest in human existential experience.[6]

In my opinion, pride of place must be given, in all these studies, to a recently published work by Max Seckler, *In-*

"La structure psychologique de l'acte de foi chez saint Thomas d'Aquin," *Freib. Zeitschr. für Phil. und Theol.* 1 (1954), 281–301; "Aspects psychologiques de l'analysis fidei chez saint Thomas d'Aquin, *ibid.* 2 (1955), 148–172, 296–315; "L'illumination de la foi chez saint Thomas d'Aquin," *ibid.* 3 (1956), 29–38; M. Labourdette, "L'affection dans la foi théologale," *RT* 43 (1937), 101–115.

For the historical background to all these studies, see G. Engelhardt, *Die Entwicklung der dogmatischen Glaubenspsychologie in der mittelalterlichen Scholastik vom Abälardstreit bis zu Philipp dem Kanzler,* Münster 1933; for later scholasticism, see F. Schlagenhaufen, "Die Glaubensgewiszheit und ihre Begründung in der Neuscholastik," *ZKT* 56 (1932), 311–379, 530–595.

For the connection between Thomas's "light of faith" and the mystical theology of John of the Cross, see Joh. a Cruce Peters, *Geloof en mystiek,* Louvain 1957.

4 For the study of Albert the Great's vision of faith, see the compelling article by A. Maccaferri, "Le dynamisme de la foi selon Albert le Grand," *RSPT* 29 (1940), 278–303.

5 For Bonaventure's vision of faith, see the rewarding book by R. Rosenmöller, *Religiöse Erkenntnis nach Bonaventura* (Beiträge, pt. XXV–3 and 4), Münster 1925, especially 94–123.

6 The representatives of that movement are, of course, universally known: J. Mourroux, G. Marcel, R. Guardini, A. Brunner, etc.

stinkt und Glaubenswille nach Thomas von Aquin,[7] the
substance of which was originally written as a thesis and
submitted by the author to the faculty of Catholic theology
at Tübingen. I can best characterise this book as a genetic
study, almost on the lines of form criticism, of the non-
conceptual aspect of the act of faith in the works of Aquinas.
And let me say at once that Seckler's study surpasses everything that we have hitherto been offered in the way of
historical and theological analysis of the grace of faith as
the basis of the entire life of faith according to Aquinas. It
seems to be that a detailed analysis of this book, providing
a basis for critical reflection, would, for various reasons, be
very valuable. In the first place, there are in this work very
important elements which must be given their rightful place
in the development of modern systematic thought about the
life of faith. Secondly, this book is important in that it brings
us, by way of a historical confrontation with Aquinas's vision
of faith, into contact with a world of thought in which a
certain contemporary sensibility in connection with the secularisation of society is manifestly expressed.

AQUINAS'S VISION OF FAITH ACCORDING
TO SECKLER

In the first part of the book (pp. 19–68), the author out-
lines the history of the word *instinctus*. He discusses the
various differences in meaning of this word and its use in
Roman and Greek literature (*instinctus* was used to trans-
late the Greek words *enthousiasmos* and *hormē*, which clearly
already had a numinous meaning), in patristic literature
and in the scholasticism of the early and high Middle Ages.
The whole field in which *instinctus* in its unity of meaning

7 Mainz 1962.

was applied in the works of Aquinas is studied against this background. He would appear to have used the word in a wide variety of applications: (a) the natural instinct, the instinct of the will, the intellect or the conscience; (b) the instinct of God or an "inward, divine instinct," an instinct of grace; (c) the instinct of the celestial bodies, of the *daimōn* and of the devil; and finally (d) the "inward, highei and special instinct," a divine instinct in many different sectors of the life of grace—the instinct of faith, the instinct in the gifts of the Holy Spirit and so on. Aquinas was aware of an *instinctus* at all levels of life. The word *instinctus* (which means something quite different from what is meant by our modern word "instinct," although all affinity cannot be excluded) sometimes had a psychological significance in Aquinas and sometimes a purely ontological, non-psychological significance. Yet, throughout the entire wide field in which Aquinas used the word, *instinctus* nonetheless has a clear unity of meaning—"instinct" is an active impulse (*sufficiens inductivum*) *de facto* suited to bring about activity in a certain sector of life. This introductory semantic study is followed by an analysis, in the three long sections of the second part of Seckler's work (pp. 69–258), of the "instinct of faith" or the grace which invites us to believe.

The Beginning of Faith according to Aquinas's Earliest Works

In the first place, the problem is situated within the context in which Aquinas discussed it—justification by faith, and thus in the wider context of a theology of conversion (*conversio,* with its remote and immediate preparation) and consequently in the broad Thomist framework of the doctrine of *exitus* and *reditus*; that is, the creative act by means of which all creatures are flowing out from God is at the

same time the principle of their return to God. Within this
context, the problem of the *initium fidei*, the beginning of
faith, is posed—how is this return brought about in man?
In this part of the book, Seckler adds nothing that is sub-
stantially new to what H. Bouillard had already put forward
in his book, *Conversion et grâce chez saint Thomas*,[8] but
unlike Bouillard Seckler concentrates his attention on the
beginning of faith. Thinking along the same lines as Bouillard, but more acutely and consistently, he makes the discovery that changes of emphasis took place between Aquinas's earlier works and his later writings. According to Seckler, Aquinas held the following view in his earlier works:
although it is ultimately God who moves our will to believe,
the will to believe nevertheless does not come about by
virtue of many different impulses or a divine instinct, but
through the medium of man's appreciation of a value. What
moves man to consent in faith is, according to Seckler's
view of the younger Aquinas, not the personal God, but
the idea of a value, the prospect of a value to which the will
aspires. And this idea of a value is based on a taking cog-
nisance of the Message of the gospels—faith comes "from
what is heard."[9] According to Seckler's interpretation, therefore, this is not directly a question of experiencing a value in
an inward attraction of grace on hearing the Good News.
The Message, presented outwardly, speaks to man and addresses an invitation to him. But this invitation only becomes a *ratio credendi*, a motive of belief, by way of rational argument, as it is only after "argumentative thought"
that it is possible and permissible to give consent in faith,
in view of the fact that it is the verification of the valuable
aspect of what is offered which in fact *makes* it a motive of

8 Paris 1944.
9 *In 3 Sent.* d. 23, q. 3, a. 4, ad 4; ad 2; d. 25, q. 2, a. 2, sol. 2, ad 3;
a. 1, sol. 5, ad 1; d. 24; q. 1, a. 3, sol. 2, ad 2.

belief. In this way, scope is also provided for the voluntary
character of faith, since, assuming that the Good News is
heard, it is always up to an initiative of man's free will to
respond or not to respond to the Word that is heard and
to accomplish the act of faith. According to Seckler, there
is in Aquinas's earliest works no question of an "actual
grace" in the making of the act of faith. The universal
dynamism of human life is sufficient, on hearing the Message of the gospels, for the acceptance of this Message as a
value in life or for its refusal as a non-value by a personal
decision.

In this argument, Seckler is at one with Bouillard, who
had already made the discovery that the Aquinas of the
Scriptum and of the *De veritate* was (like his contempo-
raries) unfamiliar with the Church's documents condemning Semi-Pelagianism, that is, the texts of the Second Council
of Orange.

The New Doctrine of "Instinct" and Its Three Sources

In a masterly analysis, on the lines of form criticism, Seckler next comes to an understanding of how Aquinas incorporated his doctrine about the *instinctus fidei* into his earlier
arguments about the *lumen fidei* (the commentary on the
Sentences, *De veritate*) and of how his theology of the act of
faith—thanks to his idea of "instinct"—thereby acquired a
completely different emphasis.

The discovery of Semi-Pelagianism: instinct as grace.
Seckler proceeds from Bouillard's correct finding that, dur-
ing his first period in Italy (1259–1260), Aquinas, either
indirectly or directly, came across the documents of the
ecclesiastical condemnation of Semi-Pelagianism. From a

36 THE VALUE OF OUR CONCEPTS OF FAITH

certain point onwards (in the middle of the period in which
he was writing his third book *Contra Gentiles*), three ideas
which are not found in Aquinas's earlier works suddenly
made an appearance in his writing: greater stress was placed
on God's initiative; an *auxilium divinum* was seen to be
directly active in the human will; and the older doctrine
of *habitus fidei*, faith as a habit, was subordinated to a more
dynamic view of justification, so that the movement of God,
the *motio divina*, came to occupy a central place. Bouillard,
whose view was later adopted by Chenu,[10] gave the following reasons for the appearance of these new ideas—Aquinas's
increasing knowledge of the later works of Augustine, his
more intensive study of the Bible and his discovery of Aristotle's *Eudemian Ethics*.

Seckler, however, goes deeper than this. It struck him particularly that the transition of Thomas's texts was quite
abrupt. The evidence of this is to be found in many different
elements, both in the terminology and in the contents of
his writing at this time. Suddenly one finds repeated refer-
ences to *pelagiani* (Semi-Pelagianism), each time connected
with a quotation from the *Eudemian Ethics* (for the first
time in *Contra Gentiles* III, c. 89, 147, 149). Bouillard, however, had not noticed that the concept *instinctus* also appeared at this very point in Thomas's works in connection
with the act of faith. And it is a remarkable fact that the
term *instinctus* played a part both in the Church's documents condemning Semi-Pelagianism and in the Latin translation of the *Eudemian Ethics*. The word *instinctus* is the
only connection that can be established in Thomas's thought
between anti-Semi-Pelagianism and these *Ethics* of Aristotle. Just as the danger of Semi-Pelagianism was averted in

10 *Introduction à l'étude de saint Thomas d'Aquin*, Montreal and Paris
1950, 236. Eng. trans., *Toward Understanding St. Thomas*, Chicago 1964,
275.

the writings of the Church Fathers by an appeal to the *instinctus divinus,* so too did this same term play a similar part centuries later in the works of Aquinas. On the basis of the Bible, the affirmation of the instinct of faith was given *scope* in Aquinas's doctrine thanks to his knowledge of the later works of Augustine, an *ontological structure* thanks to Aristotelianism and finally an *anthropological form* thanks to the Roman philosophy of law and Stoic ethics.

The new element to which prominence was given by the valorisation of the concept of *instinctus* in Thomas's teaching about faith is clearly illustrated in a text such as this: "not only has external or objective revelation the power to attract, but also an inner instinct impelling and moving to belief. . . . The Father draws many to the Son through an instinct, divine action *moving man's heart within to belief.*"[11] In this deepening of Augustine's doctrine thanks to the concept of *instinctus,* Thomas referred to three biblical texts:[12] Phil. ii. 13 ("For it is God who works in you, inspiring both the will and the deed, for his own chosen purpose"), Hos. xi. 4 (according to the Vulgate, which had the same idea of *tractus*: "in funiculis Adam traham eos in vinculis caritatis"—"with cords of man I shall draw them, and with bonds of love") and Prov. xxi. 1 ("The king's heart is a stream of water in the hand of Yahweh; he turns it wherever he will"). Hearing the Message and appreciation of the value of what has been heard (the *Scriptum, De veritate*)

---

11 ". . .non solum revelatio exterior vel obiectum, virtutem attrahendi habet, sed etiam interior instinctus impellens et movens ad credendum. . . . Trahit multos Pater ad Filium per instinctum divinae operationis *moventis interius cor hominis ad credendum.*" *Super Ev. Joa.* c. 6, lect. 5 (ed. Marietti 1952, n. 935); this is particularly apparent if this text is seen against the background of the text of Augustine that inspired it: *De spiritu et littera* 34 (*PL* 44, 240).

12 Always in the context of his commentary on John vi. 44: "No one can come to me unless the Father who sent me draws him."

were now seen to be borne up by a "divine instinct that prompts and moves us to believe." This is, as an explicit statement certainly, a *novum* in Thomas. The second part of Augustine's text ("either from without by gospel exhortations. . .or from within where no one can hinder what comes into his mind"),[13] which in Augustine had a psychological meaning, was clearly given a deeper, ontological significance by Thomas. It is evident that Thomas owed this renewed insight to a reading of Augustine against the background of the documents condemning Semi-Pelagianism (probably the *Indiculus* of Pope Celestine) which he had recently come across for the first time. Whereas Augustine had, in accordance with his neo-Platonism, seen the attraction or *tractus* of grace ("neno venit ad me, nisi Pater *traxerit* eum"— John vi. 44) as God's drawing or attraction of man by way of a recognised value, Thomas took this idea onto a deeper level. In his case, it was not only external revelation, not only the proclaimed Message of the gospels that radiated this power of attraction, but also the *instinctus interior*. In this way, he gave to the inward psychological quality of Augustine's doctrine a deeper, ontological dimension. In other words, God personally brings about in man a sensitivity towards, a state of readiness to be addressed by, the value known "from what is heard"—the Good News of the gospels. This *instinctus interior* is, however, in Aquinas himself, a purely ontological, *formal* principle.[14] Still, Aquinas

---

[13] ". . .sive extrinsecus per evangelicas exhortationes. . .sive intrinsecus, ubi nemo habet in potestate quid ei veniat in mentem." *Loc. cit.*

[14] This instinct is therefore not really something that is also psychical although not reflexive, or explicitly conscious as in the modern analyses, an *experience*. I should prefer not to discuss precisely at this point the question as to whether Thomas's doctrine, as, in my view, correctly analysed by Seckler, should not be extended by the affirmation of a non-conceptual but certainly affective conscious element that is present *as experience*.

did not do away with the inward affective aspects of Augustine's teaching, but gave them a firm substructure with his ontological "instinct of faith." In fact God's "drawing" or attraction of man took place, in his view, in many different ways—both the *Mysterium tremendum* of God's Majesty and the power of attraction proceeding from Jesus' human appearance played a part in this.[15]

The Liber de bona fortuna: *the ontological structure.* Aquinas went further with his analysis of this *instinctus interior*. His immediate source for this further ontological analysis was not the *Eudemian Ethics*, but the *Liber de bona fortuna*, which was attributed to Aristotle and contained passages from the *Eudemian Ethics*. Aquinas became familiar with this work in Italy (1259–1260), thus at about the same time that he came across the new conciliar documents. There is also a material connection—Aquinas refuted the Semi-Pelagian view of faith's beginning with arguments from this *Liber de bona fortuna*, as it is in this peripatetic *Liber* that the term *instinctus divinus* appears in the sense of a "divine instinct *bringing happiness,*" an instinct that makes man appreciate a value, and at the same time as an "instinct" that is conceived as a *moving principle (principium movens)*. These peripatetic ideas provided Thomas with all the conceptual material that he needed to valorise ontologically, in his doctrine of the *instinctus fidei*, the affirmation of the *tractus fidei*, the drawing to faith, suggested by Scripture and elaborated by Augustine.

"Whoever believes has a *sufficient motive* to believe. . .; he is prompted to believe. . .especially by an *inner instinct from God drawing him*" (II–II, q. 2, a. 9, ad 3). This inward instinct of God that invites to faith is the mainstay

15 *Super Ev. Joa.* c 6, lect 5, n. 935: "persuadendo, demonstrando et alliciendo" (by persuading, demonstrating and alluring).

of the entire act of faith. "Faith is an intellectual consent under the impulse of the human will which is moved to this (consent) by God's grace" (II–II, q. 2, a. 9). This does not mean that Thomas, bearing in mind what he had taught in his earlier works, at this stage accepted a double motive for faith—both the appreciation of a value and the divine *motio*. The inward instinct of faith, as the beginning of the entire act of faith, is a tendency of the human spirit itself, but as set in motion by the God of salvation, through which an appreciation of the value of the Message that is heard is brought into being in man.[16] It is a question of a "gift of a divine instinct bringing happiness" and a "moving principle." It brings happiness (namely, a proclamation of salvation) because "through it men are indeed fortunate, since they are inclined to what is good by a movement from God, as appears in the chapter concerning good fortune."[17] Man, after all, makes his own happiness, appreciating what is objectively valuable as a value for himself, whenever he follows the divine instinct,[18] for in the orientation of this divine instinct an objective guarantee is given to the subjective experience of this value. But this instinct is not only something that brings happiness *verum sub ratione boni*, as a right relation to the good. It is also a moving principle—it not only makes us appreciate what comes from "what is heard" as a value for life, but it is also a divine power which enables us to make the act of consent as a *human* act—which, however, transcends our human powers.

Up to this point, everything is satisfactory, and we are confronted with an astute historical analysis. But from here

16 See Seckler, 110.

17 ". . .ex hoc homines vere sunt *bene fortunati*, quod per divinam causam *inclinentur ad bonam*, ut patet in cap. de Bona Fortuna" (*In 10 Ethic.* lect. 14).

18 Seckler, 111.

onwards, reading between the lines, one begins to sense a modern problem tempting the author to "eisegesis." The instinct of faith in the sense of "moving principle" may not, Seckler claims, be regarded as an *actual grace* acting efficaciously on man. On the contrary, "human nature as a centre of action that has once been constituted is a divine counsel become nature for the purpose of the realisation of the good."[19] The instinct of faith, as an "instinct for the divine," is—as appears from Seckler's further analysis—identified with the inherent tendency of human nature (the act of which is, for example, the *desiderium naturale*) or with the human concern with the Absolute.[20] Even before man is aware of this or that value (either philosophical or theological), he is already impelled by God towards the good. This impulse, given to human nature by the divine act of creation, is, together with the evangelical Message "from what is heard," sufficient to allow man freely to decide to consent to this message and live or to reject it and die. The "instinct" has therefore to be seen as a "continuation of creation" which is, on man's side, a "tendency that has become nature." What comes from hearing—"external revelation"—therefore only actuates man's supernatural potential which is prepared by grace and is still dormant (pp. 128–129). There is in man a primordial instinct, a "sympathy," for everything that has value and importance for him. This sympathy, Seckler maintains, is not a datum of experience and has no psychological value. It has a purely ontological significance, being "given with man's essential form" (p. 135).

Stoic ethics and philosophy of law: the anthropological analysis. Seckler next makes an anthropological analysis of the instinct of faith (pp. 136 ff.). In this, the concept of

[19] P. 114, with a reference to Cajetan, *In I-II* q. 9, art 4.
[20] Thomas's commentary on 2 Cor. iii. 1: "Hoc etiam Philosophus vult..." ("This the Philosopher means...") plays an important part here.

instinctus in the early Church's condemnation of Semi-Pelagianism which was elaborated along Aristotelian lines by Aquinas is closely linked with the idea of "natural law" coming originally from Stoic sources and elaborated by Isidore of Seville and the early scholastic canonists. The ontologically interpreted *instinctus naturae*, natural instinct, was the source of many different tendencies and, via these tendencies, the basis of the "natural law."

The human intellect is the organ through which the "primordial instinct" or "primordial sympathy" is made conscious (p. 140). This primordial instinct, seen as tendency, as *forma* tending towards, is there before all consciousness and before all *de facto* will and action. In all respects, a creature is a *movens motum*—not only moves but is moved. That is its creaturely condition. But the object's appearing as a value is an indispensable condition for concrete human action. Every human act is in this way embedded in an instinct of love, in the subject's being seized, in sympathy, by values. I strive towards a value which I can appreciate as a value for myself. Every desire of the will is a dynamic consequence of an idea or *representation* of a value, but, on the other hand, only that which corresponds to a natural tendency is represented as a value. Knowledge is therefore, both prospectively and retrospectively, embedded in a dynamism of striving. Via the representation of a value the natural tendency becomes a conscious striving towards a value (pp. 143–145).

But, just as all human knowledge, "coming partly from within ... partly from without" (*De veritate* q. 19, a. 6, Seckler, p. 147), has in itself a universal, intentional scope which is, however, made particular by many different contacts with the outside world, so too do we find a double orientation in the interior instinct. The primordial instinct is a sort of "pre-evangelical climate" that is "addressed" by the Message of the gospels. The inward element is essentially directed in its intention towards that which comes from without. It is in contact with the evangelical Message as a *bonum repromissum* or Promise that the instinct of nature develops into an instinct of faith.

The primordial instinct and the instinct of faith are, however, not identical in man. The "law of grace" includes two elements—the inward element of grace and the outward communication by the revelation of the Word (II–II, q. 106, a. 1 and a. 2). Seckler calls the inward grace of faith simply a "formal openness to a sphere of reality."[21] This formal definite character which, like every *forma*, has an inherent tendency, must, however, be *interpreted* and so to speak objectively defined by what comes "from what is heard." The initially relatively undefined character of the grace of faith[22] requires the *determinatio fidei*, the contribution of the explicit content of faith, and this comes "from what is heard."[23] In the ontological sense, the tendency of the light of faith is "univocal." It is not, however, univocal in the psychological sense—in the case of one person, it is revealed in restlessness, in the case of another, in a consciousness of sin, in a dissatisfaction with the world's fulfilment of human expectations. External revelation, the evangelical Message, "informs" these uncertain, groping tendencies of man. The revelation in Word, preaching, Christianity in this way "inform" the psychologically blind instinct of faith of the "inclined heart." Inwardly illuminated in this way, "objective faith" is born in the decision of the free human will. "Be-

21 P. 153. This seems to me to be completely correct as a historical interpretation of Thomas.

22 See *In 3 Sent.* d. 24. q. 1, a. 3, sol. 3, ad 3.

23 "Fides ex auditu" ("Faith comes from hearing"); see *In 3 Sent.* d. 25, q. 2, a. 1, sol. 1; *SCG* III, c. 154; *In Ep. ad Rom.* 10, lect 2 (ed. Marietti 1953, n. 844).

lieving is the informing of a tendency" (p. 155). The reality
of salvation grasped in faith thus also possesses, as *truth,* a
relationship of finality—the saving value is accepted as truth
sub ratione boni. Believing is a "verdict guided by a value"
(p. 155), a judgment of consent contained in the appreciation of a value. The beginning of faith is situated in the
heart—"in affectione" (*De veritate,* q. 14, a. 2, ad 10).

How, then, are the two Thomist affirmations—we believe
on the authority of the God of revelation and we believe by
virtue of the appreciation of a value—related to each other?
Aquinas's answer to this is given in the context of the medieval formula, believing is "credere Deum, Deo et in Deum."
The object of faith consists of saving truths, of values for
our life, and the value of what is testified to plays a part
in the act of faith. On the other hand, the value of what
is testified to depends on the value of the witness. In God,
the witness—according to his competent authority—and
that which is testified to—according to its qualitative value
—are identical. In its root, faith is an act of salvation, an
act in which a decision is made concerning the "to be or
not to be" of our life.[24]

It is, therefore, thanks to the inward instinct of faith that
we recognise the outwardly heard Message as *conveniens,*
or as a value for life. A definite content for life, presented
or preached to us, is recognised as the answer to the deepest tendencies of the human will (p. 156). The will, which
by the dynamism of the instinct of faith is brought within
the sphere of influence of this value presented to it by hearing, draws the intellect (which, in itself and of its own
accord, proceeds along the slow path of verification and argument) along with it in the direction which the Message proposes. On this basis, the human person ultimately makes
the decision as to whether he will venture in this direction

---

[24] See M. D. Chenu, *BThom,* pt. 1 (1931–1933), 97* and the following
pages.

or not—the decision is taken and the act of faith is made or it is refused. In all this there is, therefore, no question of intuitions of faith, of affective intuitions of the content of faith. We perceive this content of faith from what is heard (we see it in the life of the Church), but it is only recognised as a value that has meaning for us because it corresponds to a tendency of the human spirit, a tendency that goes back to the living God himself.

The inner involvement of human freedom in God in the religious act is *articulated* by the word of revelation into an explicit confession of articles of faith. Who, however, provides the guarantee of the objectivity of "what is heard"? The instinct of faith does not, after all, entail any representational aspects. The "light of faith," which is identical with the "habit of faith" (p. 158), is a *principle* of knowledge in faith—it *makes something seen.*[25] But Seckler says that, according to Thomas, nothing is in fact seen in this light.[26] The light of faith makes the truth of revelation that comes from the evangelical message an authentic knowledge in faith by showing this datum "from what is heard" as valuable to whoever is confronted by the Message. In this way the light of faith brings about the act of faith in the free will.[27] It is clear from the context in which Aquinas

[25] "Lumen fidei *facit videre* ea quae creduntur" ("The light of faith *causes us to see* the things that are believed"), as Thomas repeatedly says: see II–II, q. 1, a. 4, ad 3; q. 1, a. 5, ad 1; *In 3 Sent.* d. 2, a. 1, ad 4. Seckler, however, pays no attention to these texts, but prefers to consider other texts which appear to say the "opposite."

[26]"Lumen fidei *non* facit videre illa quae creduntur" ("The light of faith does *not* cause us to see the things that are believed"); see *BT* I, q. 3, a. 1, ad 4, noting that Seckler quotes wrongly—q. 1.

[27] Nonetheless, Seckler seems not to attach very much value to the *lumen fidei.* All his attention is devoted to the *instinctus fidei.* The instinct is a *tendency,* whereas the *lumen,* of its very nature, illuminates. What is the meaning of a *light* producing a tendency? Seckler's laconic answer to this is that "this 'light' that produces a tendency has led to a great deal of ingenious guessing." I, however, welcome this matter-of-fact sobriety (pp.

again and again used the term "light of faith" that this light guarantees not a certainty based on evidence (*certitudo evidentiae*), but a firmness in consenting to a non-evident truth (*firmitas adhaesionis*). From this, it is clear that a higher value is set on the "tendency" than upon the "light."

The "light of faith" or the "habit of faith" makes man positively open towards the really revealed truths. As a natural tendency, the inclination of this habit is in itself infallible, but the specification of it by what is presented from without is fallible. In other words, errors are possible in the *interpretation* of this tendency with regard to what comes from the community. On the other hand, faith terminates in the reality of salvation itself, the God of salvation, and properly speaking not in the *enuntiabilia* or the judgments of faith as such (II-II, q. 1, a. 2, ad 2). Insofar as the believer is, by virtue of the light of faith, orientated towards the divine reality of salvation itself, this light operates infallibly. This is, however, not the case when the believer begins to explicitate this real contact in faith with God in separate affirmations of faith. In such cases of material error, faith in the existential sense remains inviolate. The absolute guarantee of infallibility in respect of separate affirmations of faith is therefore situated by Aquinas in the teaching authority of the Church (II–II, q. 5, a. 3).

The Instinct of Faith in the Dialectics of Nature and Grace

This marks the beginning of the break with Seckler's interpretation, despite my complete approval of his intention in

---

158–159). All kinds of vague and "mystical" explanations of a certain "*experience* of faith" are in circulation at present, and nobody knows what is really meant by them.

this chapter. Seckler's aim is to situate the instinct of faith in the life of historical mankind, in which he does not see the "natural" and the "supernatural" elements as divided into two levels, the one so to speak built up on the other. Grace, in his view, is not a "superstructure." Man's being is such that the beatific vision of God is "natural" to him, even though it transcends his powers and is therefore "supernatural." This is, of course, in the literal sense of the word, pure historical Thomism.[28] Whether Seckler explicitates this Thomistically, however, and whether this explicitation can —quite apart from the question as to whether it is Thomist —be theologically justified is another question, which I shall discuss later on. First of all, however, let us consider Seckler's argument.

The question which Seckler asks himself is this: Is there place for a "medium" between nature and grace? Is the instinct of faith "nature" or "grace"? It is immediately apparent that the background to this problem is Henri de Lubac's work *Surnaturel,* the difficulties of which were cleared up—this at least was the intention—by Karl Rahner and Hans Urs von Balthasar by their postulation of what they call the "supernatural existential," which is neither "human nature" in itself (in the abstract) nor "sanctifying grace." The background for Thomas himself is the affirmation of the *gratia media* in medieval Franciscan theology.

Briefly formulated, Seckler's view comes to this. God's *universal* creative activity—as continued in creation—is "converted" into a special creative activity, which is then identical with the instinct of faith, whenever it comes into contact with man, who, as a spiritual being, is by his very

28 See *BT* I, q. 2, a. 4, ad 5: "Quamvis homo *naturaliter* inclinetur in finum ultimum, non tamen potest naturaliter illum consequi, *sed solum per gratiam.*" ("Though man is *naturally* inclined to his last end, yet he cannot attain it naturally, *but only by grace.*")

nature "receptive to grace." This occurs because of the special structure of this receiving subject, man. The divine activity which moves men towards natural and supernatural values is in itself one and the same—it is neither "natural" nor "supernatural," because in itself it can "scarcely be qualitatively defined" (p. 192). It is defined by that on which it has an effect, which is, in this case, human nature. Man's constitutive orientation, as a spiritual being, towards grace is therefore the explanation for the fact that God's creative activity in man becomes an instinct impelling and moving him to believe.[29] Faced with a spiritual being, the divine action, without which no creaturely activity is conceivable, is at the same time a *gratia oblata*, and offer of grace. Faced with the God of creation, various participations in the one *motio divina* (creative activity) take place in and because of the structure of man's being. As a result of this, the *motio divina* is known sometimes as the "natural instinct," drawing us to faith, and finally as the instinct of grace. This is why, in its spiritual core, human nature is in principle a *promise of grace*. The instinct of nature becomes in the concrete sense a "gratia operans et praeveniens." *Concrete* human nature is itself a "call to grace," an instinct that impels us towards faith. That is, in Seckler's view, why Thomas, reacting against Semi-Pelagianism, did not incorporate a new supernatural instinct into human nature, but rather analysed the dynamism of human nature in the concrete. It is in any case clear that the instinct of faith is not identical with the state of grace; it is an *invitation* to this justification, a divine aid. This aid moves by stimulating; but this, in the concrete, means nothing other than the "transcendental movement of the creature towards the good, thanks to God" (p. 178). It is not "actual grace," nor is it

29 See p. 191. " 'Vocation' refers to the help of God moving and exciting the mind interiorly" (I–II, q. 113, a. 1, ad 3).

"sanctifying grace," but rather "that movement of God which sets up in man the inner dimension of return" (*loc. cit.*). In continuing creation, God does not act on a creature that is already provisionally in existence—the entire evolutive mode of being and mode of being active is rather in a state of being created by God. Apart from sinfulness, which brings about confusion in everything, the human tendency towards the Absolute is the *divine* call that prompts us to *believe*, to give ourselves in faith to the one Being who can satisfy this natural openness. It is in this that the "remote preparation for grace" is, in Seckler's view, situated in Aquinas's later works. (See pp. 193–195.) It is in the *instinct of nature* that the ontological law for the transcendence of this nature is situated. Because of the inward orientation of nature towards the supernatural, there is, *beside* and *in* the instinct of nature, no need for a new divine impulse which would then be called an "instinct impelling to believe." "It is not in human nature to have faith; but it goes with human nature that man's mind does not reject the interior instinct and the external preaching of truth."[30]

Man's essential *being* is, viewed theologically, itself *a divine invitation to believe*, a possibility which, on hearing the evangelical Message, is freely accepted or culpably refused. As "pure man," man is "damned" (p. 200). Apart from all *gratia media* (a kind of means of linking the "natural" and the "supernatural"), man is, because of his spiritual being, orientated towards the supernatural. This finds clear expression in the natural desire. Aquinas did not look for the distinction between the natural and the supernatural —by means of which the gratuitous character of grace is

---

30 ". . .instinctus impellens ad credendum." "Habere fidem non est in natura humana: sed in natura humana est, ut mens hominis non repugnet interiori instinctui et exteriori veritatis praedicationi." II–II, q. 10, a. 1, ad 1.

saved—in a distinction between "abstract" human nature and "concretely historical" human nature (the direction followed by Rahner, Urs von Balthasar and others), but "through an ontology of first and second causality with regard to the creaturely spiritual being as an aptitude for transcendence" (p. 207).

It would certainly be possible to say all this if man were not in fact destined for divine life. It follows directly from a "transcendental analysis of the human spirit." The theologian, however, goes further. The human spirit is not changed by its *de facto* supernatural destiny. In the concrete the *instinctus interior*, man's "primordial instinct," becomes the *vehicle* of the divine vocation and destiny, for there is always a formal distinction between "man who is *capable of being called* and man who *is* called" (p. 212). The antithesis between "nature and grace" then becomes the correlation between "creation" and "covenant," the order of nature unto grace becomes an ordination. In concrete experience, it is therefore impossible to determine what is natural and what is supernatural in this *instinctus interior;* from the very first moment of man's existence, this existence is one that has been called to grace, and not simply a "request for grace." And, as a correlative to this *de facto* divine vocation to grace, something real must be present on man's side, something that is *more* in comparison with the natural capacity for grace—the reality of the factual state of being called (p. 213). What is more, this reality "must be a positive element in man's essential constitution, it must be *of grace, without actually being grace*" (*loc. cit.*). Rahner and von Balthasar see this reality in the "supernatural existential" (pp. 213–214), and, although he is not opposed to this view, Seckler does find it difficult to define the meaning of Balthasar's "existential" in this context. It is meant to point to the *obligatory* character of this destiny, although this concrete destiny cannot be a constitutive element of the essential being of human nature, but at most of man's "concrete being." Thomas, however, looks elsewhere for the solution to this problem. According to him, the structure of concrete man is no different from that of man who is possibly not called. The vocation remains therefore "extrinsic" to man—it is *God's will* that concrete man should be destined to receive grace. It is through God's "external" saving will that the "good of nature" thereby (allowing for the divine purpose) acquires a "new" meaning as a negative disposition towards the infusion of grace. In this way, the vocation is made internal without human nature being subjected to any change.

The divine vocation is communicated to man not only in verbal revelation but also "inwardly." This "inner vocation" prepares the ontological dimension (the *instinctus naturae*) by means of which man is made capable of listening to the Message. It is not human nature as nature, but the ontological *instinctus* that is the vehicle of this divine vocation (pp. 214–215). Although this "inward instinct" is a gratuitous gift, it nonetheless belongs to "nature" (p. 215). The ontological finality of the *instinctus naturae* remains hidden from man so long as it is not *interpreted* by verbal revelation. As borne up by the God of creation who wills man's salvation, this natural primordial dynamism of man is at the same time an offer of grace. The one divine movement which leads all creatures, according to their innate character, back to their origin—which, in other words, "leads them home"—is given, in man's *spirit,* the name of "grace."

Man is, however, in fact a sinner and this conferment of grace thus becomes a justifying (p. 217 ff.). In the concrete, what is proposed to the instinct is the "grace of justification as an offer" (p. 218). It is thus sanctifying grace, not as a possession and appropriated in the act of justification, but as an *offer* to be accepted. One and the same grace both calls and justifies ("grace infused, grace gained," I–II, q. 113, a. 8, ad 2).

This ontological instinct which, subject to God's vocation, is concretely an "instinct of faith" is operative in all kinds of psychological phenomena. Man is constantly coming across this divine offer of grace—it is his inescapable and fundamental human situation, even if he has not yet been confronted historically with the mystery of Christ (II–II, q. 89, a. 6). The psychological phenomena which have their most profound basis in this primordial instinct are of two kinds—the phenomenon of "restlessness," dissatisfaction with the finite, man's experience as a deficient, imperfect being and, on the other hand, his experience of a kind of orientation, resulting from his real (or supposed) discovery of the Absolute. All these elements can be found scattered about Aquinas's works. Man is a "paradox"—capable of encountering the personally Infinite, he is constantly meeting with finite things. His transcendental openness and his condition as a captive within this world form the basis of the highly characteristic "metaphysical restlessness" which either "afflicts" human life or positively "raises" it up. What we have to do with here is an "existential restlessness." Anxiety, wonder, questioning and still more questioning—these are the repeated effects, in our wordly situation, of the "primordial instinct" which is concretely a divine instinct moving and impelling man to believe. There is not a kind of "special organ" in man, as though there were a separate "religious sense" in him. It affects the whole of man and in it is revealed the "sacral character of being" (p. 224). The *instinctus interior* is therefore the source of all religiousness—that is, of man's involvement with the divine.

In the last part of his book, Seckler analyses the saving significance of the *instinctus interior* in connection with

the opportunity of salvation for those to whom the gospel
is not preached.

In conclusion, Seckler says: "God did not create the will
to believe and to be saved *in* man. Rather, he created a
man whose disposition towards the path of salvation is situated in the cradle of his nature. It is therefore pointless to
enquire whether the grace of faith begins in the intellect or
the will. It does not enter from outside into a psychology
that is already functioning, but is given in that root of man's
being in which distinctions become meaningless" (p. 261).
In this way, Seckler himself provides an accurate summary
of his intention in this "third section" of his book: "the
instinct of nature is the *promulgated* will of God" (p. 264)
and for this reason the *instinctus interior* is the "relationship
of the subject to itself as due-to-be and due-to-be-such" (p.
264). In this perspective, faith is the bringing to fulfilment
of a tendency which is prior to the hearing of the Message,
but which only comes to itself in the listening to this gospel.
That fundamental freedom created by the God of salvation
which is man is a state of being called—an "offer of grace"
which man must faithfully substantiate in himself. The
content of faith is connected with this state of being called.
"This instinct is, according to Thomas, the effective and
sufficient inward cause for faith and salvation" (p. 261).
The will to believe is therefore not a decision brought about
by actual grace to enable man to regard a number of truths
"as true," but the ethical expression of an ontological law,
made concrete in confrontation with an actual historical
Message. The instinct of faith is not a privilege of some men
who in fact believe, but the vehicle of God's mercy directed
towards all men. Aquinas thus provided the medieval doctrine of faith, which was above all psychologically orientated
and owed its inspiration to Augustine, with an *ontological
substructure* by the theological discovery of the *instinctus*

fidei. In this way, he also gave this doctrine an *anthropological* extension.

CRITICAL REVIEW

In the foregoing section I have provided at least a broad outline of Aquinas's view of faith in accordance with Max Seckler's accurate—though sometimes amplificatory—analysis of Aquinas's texts. Since Seckler's book is primarily a historical analysis, we should not be daunted by the word *instinctus*. It would be right for a modern study of faith to avoid this word, as "instinct" and "religion" call quite different notions to the mind of modern man, and, what is more, the word *instinctus* (*motio*) is no longer appropriate to a more personally oriented view. But we are after all concerned with Aquinas's view of faith, and he was bound to express himself in the language of his time. First of all, let us briefly summarise this view.

Aquinas's View of Faith

Commenting on the well-known text of St. John, "All that the Father gives me will come to me" (John vi. 37). Thomas says: "What we should notice in this text is that not only the *habitus* must be included in this gift—that is, faith and so on—[31] but also the inner impulse to believe. For everything that he does for salvation is, in its entirety, a gift of God" (*Super Ev. Joa.* c. 6, lect. 4). By virtue of the *instinctus fidei (gratia operans)* or the *initium fidei,* man makes himself receptive towards this invitation (which thus becomes *gratia cooperans* in the act of reception) on hearing

[31] Thomas means the *lumen fidei,* which is precisely the *habitus* of faith (*In 3 Sent.* d. 23, q. 2, a. 1, ad 4).

the Message of the gospels. Two characteristic texts may serve to illustrate this: "For faith two things are required: one is an inclination of the heart towards belief, and this does not come from hearing, but from the gift of grace; the other is decision as to what is to be believed, and this does come from hearing"[32]; and "The calling of man is twofold; one is exterior, through the mouth of a preacher. The other is interior, it is simply an instinct of the mind, by which a man's heart is moved by God to assent to those things which are of faith or virtue."[33] According to Thomas, this inner vocation or the *instinctus fidei* was a *tractio Patris,* a drawing by the Father (*Super Ev. Joa.* c. 6, lect. 5), which, through the man Jesus in the power of the Spirit, inwardly invites the man who hears the Message of the gospel in his freedom to surrender to this Message and to the reality of salvation. The *tractio Patris* comes to us via Christ,[34] but Christ does this by virtue of the Holy Spirit.[35]

---

[32] "Ad fidem duo requiruntur: quorum unum est cordis inclinatio ad credendum et hoc non est ex auditu, sed ex dono gratiae; aliud autem est determinatio de credibili, et istud est ex auditu" (*In Ep. ad Rom.* 10, 17, lect 2).

[33] "Vocatio hominis est duplex: una exterior, quae fit ore praedicatoris. Alia vero vocatio est interior, quae nihil aliud est quam quidam mentis instinctus, quo cor hominis movetur a Deo ad assentiendum his quae sunt fidei vel virtutis" (*In Ep. ad Rom. 8,* 30, lect. 6).

[34] See *Quodl.* 2, q. 4, a. 1, ad 3: "Interior instinctus quo Christus poterat se manifestare sine miraculis exterioribus, pertinet ad virtutem veritatis primae quae interius hominem illuminat et docet" ("The inner instinct by which Christ was able to show himself for what he was without external miracles pertains to the virtue of primary truth which illumines and teaches a man from within").

[35] See *Super Ev. Joa.* 14, lect. 6: "Nisi Spiritus Sanctus adsit cordi audientis, otiosus est sermo doctoris, . . .et in tantum quod etiam ipse Filius Dei organo humanitatis loquens non valet, nisi ipsemet interius operetur per Spiritum Sanctum" ("Unless the Holy Spirit is in the hearer's heart, the teacher's word is fruitless. . .to the point that even the Son of God speaking with human mouth is unavailing unless he himself is worked upon

The act of faith is based entirely on this inner vocation as on its unique foundation. In consenting to this inner vocation, man attains, supernaturally but in and through the inclination of his own heart, to the divine testimony on which he relies exclusively in order to accept the Message that he has heard (even though a rational verification of faith will also normally protect him here from any possible pseudo-experience). But this faith is not supported by any reasoning about God, who cannot deceive, but only by the inner experience of the concrete testimony of God's authority. This is an experience that the message heard "is good for me"—the beliver "knows how good it is for him to give himself in this way to the truth of faith" (*De Divinis Nominibus* c. 7, lect. 5). Seckler says that the light of faith is a *formal* principle of knowing which manifests the Message heard as relevant (cf. p. 160), but he does not say what its relevance in fact is. Developing Seckler's notion and, in any case, "interpreting Thomistically," I would clarify this in the following way. The relevance in question here is the relevance as *revelation*, in other words, the aspect of "being testified to by God"—what comes to us "from what is heard" is *de facto* supremely relevant as said to me by God, and thus as divine revelation, by virtue of the *instinctus* of the light of faith. If then the light of faith, through its *instinctus*, invests the Message heard with relevance for me, this means that I attain to the truth of salvation held out to me, *precisely* (and *only*) in and through this divine instinct, *in the sense of* "truth revealed by God." In the light of faith I thus come to the "formal motive" of faith, and I therefore perceive the Message to be a personal message from God to

---

inwardly by the Holy Spirit"). We can therefore call the instinct of faith an *instinctus Spiritus Sancti* (III, q. 36, a. 5; *In 4 Sent.* d. 13, q. 1, a. 2, sol. 1), although in these texts it is a question of divine impulses not directly towards faith, but to special acts of faith by believers.

me. I am, however, bound to admit, with Seckler, that the light of faith as such is, according to Aquinas's texts themselves, a purely formal *principle* of knowing that is informed by the "datum from what is heard," which is itself illuminated by this "inclusion" in the light of faith (it is, in this sense, invested with relevance).

The New Elements in Seckler's Analysis

What is distinctive in Seckler's book, in contrast to the view of the fundamental meaning of the grace of faith (*instinctus fidei*) that has been current for a long time, especially in Thomist circles, is to be found first of all in his genetic elucidation of Aquinas's recourse to *instinctus*. This genetic explanation, conducted almost on the lines of form criticism, seems to me to be flawless. The other new element in his analysis is his integration of this instinct of faith into Aquinas's general view of the relationship between nature and supernature. But it is precisely in the face of this explanation—which was intended by Seckler himself to set out aspects of Aquinas's texts which were merely implicit—that several questions have occurred to me. The fact that Aquinas is asked questions arising from a modern approach to problems (set in motion by Maréchal, de Finance, de Lubac, Heidegger and others)—questions which Aquinas did not ask explicitly himself—and that Aquinas is made to answer these questions from his own texts does not seem to me to be an improper procedure in itself. On the contrary, even though it carries the danger of eisegesis with it, it seems to me perfectly legitimate. To think theologically is always to think with others. We should not only be concerned with what Aquinas, for example, thought, but with the one *reality* which confronted Aquinas and which also confronts us centuries later. What is more, the study of history is not

simply the making of a photocopy of the thought of someone
who has been dead for a long time. It is at the same time
also a *thinking together with him* about the problems raised
by him.[36] I do not, therefore, think any the worse of Seckler
for making an analysis that often explicitates Aquinas's implicit thought (after his analysis of Aquinas's purely historical, explicit affirmations).

The question is, however, whether Seckler has accurately
hit upon Aquinas's implicit idea in the explicitating analysis
of the third section of part two of his book (pp. 171ff.; the
third section is also to some extent anticipated in the second
section). I feel bound to say that everything would seem to
point to this, and yet I am afraid that Seckler ultimately
fails to appreciate Aquinas as a *doctor gratiae*. It is, however, not easy to situate this failure without doing Seckler
an injustice. On the one hand, he says that the *instinctus
naturae* and the *instinctus fidei* are identical—that is, materially—whereas, on the other hand, he recognises the existence of a formal distinction between them. There is certainly—according to Seckler as well—a formal distinction
between man's ability to be addressed by God (*capacitas
gratiae*) and his actual *destiny* and concrete *vocation* to the
supernatural order of life. The natural *"ordo* ad gratiam"
is, as such, not an *"ordinatio* naturae ad gratiam." In principle, Seckler is on safe Christian ground here. His orthodoxy
as a *believer* is therefore in no way in question.[37] Despite
this clear formal distinction, however, Seckler nonetheless
maintains that this *ordo* is in actual fact an *ordinatio* (a

36 There is always still an appeal to modern man in the thought of a
philosopher or a theologian who has been dead for a long time. The significance of the past changes with the new light that the present is always
throwing on it.

37 It is well to say this explicitly, because sometimes theologians suppose
—wrongly—that when their thinking on some point is challenged the
orthodoxy of their faith is being questioned.

real destiny), purely by virtue of God's saving will, without changing inwardly because of this. Man's positive but passive openness to grace belongs to his essential being. But, *in itself and of its own accord,* this is not yet a real vocation to the supernatural order—it is not a destiny in actual fact (Seckler admits this). This actual destiny is concretely contained in God's act of creation, and it is for this reason that Seckler believes that he can conclude that *concretely* the *ordo naturae ad gratiam* or (in Aquinas's *natura* terms) the *instinctus naturae* is an *instinctus fidei,* an offer of grace and an invitation to believe. Materially, nothing is changed, yet the normal openness of the human spirit to the Absolute becomes, through *this* creation, not only a quest for grace (which belongs to the essential being of our humanity), but also a concrete *offer* of grace, a grace which in fact already prompts us to make the act of faith. "Nature" is a concrete offer of grace, not on the basis of its having been created, but on the basis of its having been created by a God *of salvation.*

What I especially welcome in this solution is the care which the author takes not to situate man's *factual* state of being destined to the supernatural order in a kind of "intermediary" between nature and supernature, as Rahner and von Balthasar have tried to do, reacting against de Lubac. But an intermediary or "linking reality" of this kind is useless and in itself meaningless, because the problem of the relationship between nature and supernature is in this way only transferred to the relationship between nature and this "intermediary," which is not natural and yet is not sanctifying grace either. But with this agreement with Seckler's deepest intention, my agreement with Seckler, both as an exegete of Thomas and *secundum rei veritatem* (which is the most important consideration), must end. Both Seckler and the originators of the "supernatural existential" have, in my opinion, been led astray by an illusion of perspective, that is, by the fact that the sinner also continues to be really called and to live in a supernatural order. This is why Rahner and von Balthasar try to establish, as the term of God's saving destiny, a reality even for those who are not in grace, the "intermediary" of the supernatural existential in human nature, whereas, Seckler, leaving human nature simply nature, calls *this* nature *concretely* the term of God's saving destiny.

Let us, however, first of all clear up a misunderstanding, for in this way it will become apparent that Seckler has certainly seen something that is important. Within the framework of Aquinas's philosophy of *nature,* the *instinctus naturae* does really go out to the absolute good and therefore to the beatific vision of God, although it cannot reach this under its own power. We only know this, however, by reflection (*discretio rationis*). Man's actual orientation towards God in himself does not, in any case, take place "mechanically"—it is a *free action* on man's part.[38] It is only through the mediation of the concrete representation of God as a value that the *instinctus naturae* is, according to Aquinas, impelled towards God. Does this mean that the *instinctus naturae* is, together with the representation of the evangelical Message as a value, sufficient to provide the *instinctus naturae* with the sense of an *instinctus fidei*? This cannot be claimed even on the basis of Aquinas's implicit ideas. Aquinas was, after all, too deeply convinced that, however open man might be, as a spirit, to receive grace, his spirit was itself completely powerless to take even one step in the direction of grace. The positive quest for grace, which this spirit is, does not, in his view, signify a real offer of grace. What it does signify for him is that, if God offers grace, this grace

---

38 See *Verit.* q. 28, a. 4, ad 2: "Illud ad quod homo trahitur, aliquo modo ad liberum arbitrium pertinet."

is not a "foreign body" in our life, but meaningful to human life; indeed that it is only this grace that makes human life *personally* meaningful. In this sense, the supernatural is, for Aquinas, already visible in our human state, but simply as a distantly visible horizon. It is in the spirit that the religious life is born.

Aquinas does not ask himself explicitly whether even the natural "desire for God" is an expression in the concrete of God's saving will. This is, of course, a modern question, but it may be possible, from this modern approach to the problem (which has been raised especially since Baius), to ask Aquinas this question. If we do this, then we find that, in Aquinas's view, concrete man (the *natura instituta*) was created only in order to achieve beatific communion with God. This does not, however, mean that the *instinctus naturae* itself has become a concrete offer of grace. Man's complete helplessness in the theological sphere imposes an impassable barrier here. Man's state as a spirit is as such not an *offer of grace*. It is not even a *promise* of grace in the real sense of the word. Aquinas therefore makes a clear distinction between the desire for God on the basis of the *instinctus naturae* that we freely explicitate, by a *discretio rationis* from our own conscious being in this world, in the direction of God,[39] and the real offer of grace that enables us, in a completely new manner, to take our first step towards God.[40]

That *in God* the act of creation (by means of which God calls man's spiritual dynamism into existence and continues

[39] *In 4 Sent.* d. 49, q. 1, a. 3, sol. 3, ad 1; *Verit.* q. 22, a. 7; these and many other texts are not mentioned by Seckler.

[40] This is very marked in *In Ep. II ad Cor.* c. 5, lect. 2, where the distinction is clearly made between God as the *auctor desiderii naturalis* (the author of natural desire) and God as the *auctor desiderii supernaturalis* (the author of supernatural desire). The second is only possible, not on a basis of the instinct of nature but by the *infusion* of a supernatural spirit, that is, the Holy Spirit."

to sustain it) is identical with his act of salvation (by means
of which he calls this dynamic and open spirit to intersubjective communion with himself) does not bring us any
nearer to a solution of the problem as to how this "move·
ment" on God's part is in fact accomplished in man. It
cannot, however, mean that the *instinctus naturae* is therefore *concretely* an *instinctus fidei*. There is certainly a distinction between man's natural *"finalisation"* (as a spirit
or person) towards personal communion with God and what
he is actually being destined for. The finalisation is essentially contained in the creation of a formally spiritual being.
Being destined, on the other hand, is an act of salvation and
therefore an offer of grace. I wonder whether the two interpretations—Seckler's "naturalising" tendency on the one
hand, and Rahner's and von Balthasar's appeal to a "supernatural existential" that is distinct both from "nature" and
from "grace" on the other—do not in fact lose sight of one
simple fact. That is that the term (in man) of real *destination* for the supernatural order is precisely sanctifying grace
itself, in other words, a man's real situation in a supernatural
order, either in the mode of acceptance (sanctifying grace or
real intersubjective union with God) or in the mode of
refusal (the real condition of sinfulness). Why, then, look
for another reality—a "linking" reality like the supernatural
existential, or a bold solution identifying the offer of grace
with our humanity, which is only a powerless call for grace?
As a reality in man, man's being destined to the supernatural
order is nothing but the fruit of this *efficacious* saving will
of God—the *de facto* state of being admitted into God's
friendship or, in the case of the man who is not in a state
of grace, his *real* condition of sinfulness. In God, there is no
difference between a project and its execution. The destination itself is effective, that is, it constitutes the covenant between God and man. A reality *in* man which, being neither

"nature" nor "grace" nor "historical nature," is supposed to be the term of the supernatural destination, as a preliminary (at least according to logical priority) to the real gift of grace, is quite unacceptable. Seckler's proposition that man's factual being destined supernaturally, as a reality *in* man, is "of grace, without actually being grace" (p. 213) seems to me to be the fundamental error, not only of Seckler's entire argument, but also of Rahner's and that of von Balthasar.

The openness of the human spirit of God, man's receptivity to grace, does not suddenly become, by means of a purely extrinsic divine decree, a concrete offer of grace. This decree—God's saving will—is God's offering of himself to receptive man who, precisely by virtue of this offer, is enabled *de facto* to accept this offer and to enter into the Covenant. *In* man himself, the real offer of sanctifying grace is not only formally but also materially something quite different from his spiritual openness to the absolute and to everything dynamic that may result from this, although this "quite different" element is certainly geared to this openness. I am, of course, bound to admit that, outside the revelation in word, man has no explicit and conscious awareness, in his living experience, of any difference between what derives from the transcendental openness of his spirit (or, to use Aquinas's terms, the *instinctus naturae*) and what derives concretely from God's invitation in grace (Aquinas's *instinctus fidei*). But to identify the one with the other and to save the distinction simply by affirming that the Creator is the God of the Covenant strikes me as a failure to understand the transcendence of grace precisely *in* man. This is the fateful consequence of Seckler's failure to consider, after his very accurate analysis of Aquinas's concept of *instinctus,* Aquinas's very important and closely related concept of *voluntas ut natura,* together with his identification of the *instinctus naturae* in man with a preconscious tendency of nature in a direction which elicits all kinds of psychological phenomena from man in his contact with the world.

God's Continuous Act of Creation

I suspect, however, that Seckler still has ammunition to spare and takes recourse to the idea of *creatio continua*. What he will say is that the *instinctus naturae* becomes concretely an *instinctus fidei* by virtue of God's continuous act of creation, and he would appear to have Aquinas on his side here. It is, after all, a known fact that Aquinas equated the *exitus* from God with the "natural order" and the *reditus* (of spiritual beings) to God with the order of grace.[41] Now God's activity in leading back is nothing but his continuous creation. Seckler's interpretation of this is that the continuous act of creation, by means of which God takes his creature to its final goal (*conversio*), makes the *instinctus naturae* an instinct of faith. In this, however, he forgets that Aquinas was not asking himself the modern question which arises in this connection, because the gratuitous character of grace was not a problem in the Middle Ages and was presupposed in all cases.

According to Seckler, the act of continuous creation itself is the grace of conversion (*reditus, conversio*) in the religious sense. Since there is in man a natural tendency to transcend himself (this is in fact the real nature of his spiritual being), God's *creatio continua de facto* gives this self-transcendence, in Seckler's view, to man. But this is quite beyond my comprehension! I can only see that man, despite his humanising activity in making history, comes by the continuous act of creation precisely to the concrete experience of his own lack of power to transcend himself

[41]See, for example, *In 1 Sent.* d. 14, q. 2, a. 2; d. 15, q. 4, a. 1; see also *De Sacramentele Heilseconomie*, pt. 1, Antwerp 1952, especially 10.

by his own efforts. Man's actual transcendence of himself (in the sense of a trans-ascendence) cannot therefore be explained in terms of the *instinctus naturae*.

It is, of course, true that God's concrete saving will, the act of conferring grace, is of its very nature a *divine* act—that is, an absolute act—and this always means a "creating from nothing." The conferment of grace itself implies an act of creation and therefore an aspect of continuous creation. In other words, in the conferment and reception of grace, even to the point of the beatific encounter with God, God remains the creator and the recipient of grace remains a creature. While God draws man intimately into his friendship, this movement still contains an element of creation, which puts a distance between God and man. But the conferment of grace is more than creation, and for this reason the one who receives grace is more than a man—he is a son of God. The fullness of human life is in fact superhuman—it is divine life in a human subject. And however much we may stress that grace is an *inward* fulfilment of human life, we should all the more place full emphasis on the fact that this life-fulfilment is a transcendent completion of our humanity. This is naturally implied in the essence of Christianity as a self-transcendence by virtue of grace. Nonetheless, we do at the same time find, *in* this self-transcendence, the best of ourselves included as an additional gift. Nature and grace are thus, in their existential unity, still distinct.

In creation, God constitutes a creature, as participation of God, in its own value. In conferring grace, however, he gives *himself* as a gift to man (this divine giving being, once again, naturally a creative giving). The conferment of grace is the divine—and therefore creative—act, by means of which man is drawn into an intersubjective, theologal relationship with the living God. (This is the formal element in the act of conferring grace; the created quality, *gratia creata,* is nothing but the necessary divine mode of this act.) That is why the initiative in grace which draws us into this inter-subjective relationship cannot, even at the first stage of real offer, be materially identical with the dynamism of our human spirit itself. It is, on the contrary, a question of our being personally taken hold of by the God of salvation who reveals himself inwardly (and outwardly) to us (that is, *to* our transcendental openness) in an act that is at the same time creative, so that we experience—however confusedly—*in ourselves* this divine invitation while hearing the Message that is held out to us. It cannot take place in the manner suggested by Seckler, that is, God's one creative activity (*creatio continua*) being determined *by* the real nature of our humanity—in other words, by our spiritual being, and being "formed" into a saving activity, the gratuitous character of which is only to be found in the gratuitous nature or freedom of the act of creation itself.

We certainly ought not to regard the invitation in grace, distinct though it may be from the dynamism of our human spirit, either as extrinsic or as a physical impulse. We are addressed, in the divine invitation to faith, by Someone who is the inner, absolute ground of our existence, *interior intimo meo,* "more intimate to me than I to myself." The experience of God *as* God—this is exclusively the definition of the beatific vision of God (and even then the divine gesture which puts a distance between God and man because it is a creative gesture is still present in the very act of eschatological self-revelation). In this sense, every direct intuition of God's testimony of himself, however confused, must be totally rejected as the basis of our faith. God's testimony of himself is experienced *in ourselves.* We experience grace where we experience our humanity, and where we experience our humanity, we also concretely experience grace, because we are confronted in our freedom with grace-God, that is, with the divine saving will which is actively concerned with us. What we ultimately *experience* is only our human existence that is personally addressed by God and informed by grace—we are associated with God himself only *in faith*. We do not experience God's speaking to us in itself—since this is God himself—but as a reality in our life. That is why we cannot, *outside the revelation in Word*, distinguish grace from nature—that is, from human life. The spiritual subject that comes into contact with God in faith is a physical subject and, what is more, its physical nature is *terrestrial*. This means that grace is, in all its aspects and dimensions, entirely bound up with our life in this world. We know thematically and reflectively that nature is not grace, but this is not *distinct* in our living experience.

If this had indeed been what Seckler intended to affirm, then I should have agreed entirely with his argument—he was, after all, just in front of a door which would have given him a far better access to the mystery of grace than the door that von Balthasar had opened. But his intention was precisely to affirm, thematically and reflectively, the identity between the *instinctus naturae* and the *instinctus fidei*, and Thomist spirituality (and perhaps even Dominican spirituality as a whole), the mainstay of which has always been the primacy and the gratuitous nature of grace even though it has always held dear the idea that *gratia supponit naturam*, can only reply to this with a simple *non possumus*.

The Twofold Application of the Concept of Instinctus Interior

The significance of Aquinas's term *instinctus interior* plays a very important part in Seckler's interpretation. In itself, this concept has a neutral meaning, covering a wide field—

it can be applied to the lowest and to the highest inward forms of dynamism, to natural and to supernatural forms. The concrete meaning of the term is determined by the context. This does not mean that, since both the dynamism of the human spirit and the *initium fidei* are called an *instinctus interior*, it is possible to identify the two *realities* because of this semantic unity of meaning. In fact, Seckler fails in his interpretation of Aquinas simply because he confuses the unity of meaning of a word with the field to which it can be applied.[42] When he uses the term *instinctus divinus interior*, Aquinas always alludes to one and the same divine, and therefore creative, activity. This activity is purely creative if it is concerned with the creative preservation of the *natura*. It is, on the other hand, the divine mode of the activity of grace if it is concerned with the divine preservation (or bringing into existence) of the life of grace.

It is a pity that Seckler, who has gone so carefully into the history of the word *instinctus*, did not also do equally careful research into the term *lumen*, because this provides the real indication of the difference between *instinctus naturae* and *instinctus fidei*. It is precisely this "light" which points to the transcendent character of grace, and it is the "divine instinct" which points to the one absolute divine activity which preserves either the life of nature (*natura humana, lumen naturale*) or the life of grace (*lumen infusum*). There are irrefutable texts to be found again and again in support of this in the single article of *In Boethium de Trinitate* I, q. 1. The meaning of *operatio divina* and *novi luminis additio* is clearly apparent in this article, and also from ad 1, ad 2, ad 6 and ad 7 of this article, where

---

42 A. Reichling's book, *Het Woord. Een studie omtrent de grondslag van taal en taalgebruik*, Nijmegen 1935, would have drawn Seckler's attention to this frequently occurring confusion.

there is reference to *instinctus divinus* as against the *novum lumen*. According to Seckler, the one neutral movement of God (*instinctus interior*) becomes an *instinctus fidei* by virtue of the real nature of the *forma* which is grasped by this divine movement, in other words, the *forma humana* that is "open to God." It is by the nature of this specifically human openness that the one neutral divine movement is inwardly specified as an instinct of faith. This may well be Molinism, but it is certainly not an authentic interpretation of Aquinas.

Seckler loses sight of the fact that the *forma inhaerens,* with which we have to do in connection with the instinct of faith, is not the *forma humana,* but the new *forma* (that is already accepted or at least offered), in other words, the "light of faith." It is in any case quite clear from the texts of *In Boethium de Trinitate* mentioned above (to give only one example) that the single activity that is creative because it is divine—the activity that is always called *instinctus interior* or *motio divina* in respect of creaturely (either natural or supernatural) activity—is called *actual grace* if (to use Aquinas's words) it directly takes hold of (or offers) the new *lumen infusum,* but is a purely natural *motio divina* insofar as it takes hold of the *lumen naturale (natura humana)* as such. In other words, the meaning of the divine *instinctus interior* points as such only to the creative mode of God's activity, and does not of itself indicate whether it is a question of a divine act in connection with man's natural or his supernatural life. The *instinctus fidei* is therefore a divine creative act (*instinctus interior*) as a dimension of or as the divine mode of an *act of the conferment of grace* (that is, the *infusio luminis fidei vel gratiae* or its preservation), whereas the *instinctus naturae* is an *instinctus divinus* in connection with continuous creation of the *gu-*

bernatio.[43] It is a question of what God's activity brings
about (or what is creatively borne up by his activity)—a
natural or a saving value. Thus, man's secular, humanising
activity (as an aspect of the concrete *conversio ad Deum*) is
equally borne up by a divine *instinctus interior,* but this
should not therefore be identified with the religious *conversio* which only takes place by virtue of an offer of grace
(and thus also by a divine *instinctus interior,* since this is
just the absolute manner of God's activity). In the one case,
the *instinctus interior* is a divine offer of creaturely values.
In the second case, it is an offer of supernatural values (of a
lumen novum).

If the idea of the *lumen* is lost sight of, then, there is
every chance that the *instinctus naturae* and the *instinctus
fidei* will be identified, because the *instinctus divinus* as
such points only to the divine and therefore creative activity
either in the natural order or in the order of grace. It
therefore seems to me to be quite consistent that Seckler
(and indeed Bouillard as well), after having devoted his
attention exclusively to the *instinctus interior* of faith and
having devoted only a few pages to the *lumen fidei,* should
inevitably conclude by identifying the grace of faith as an

---

43 See *BT* I, q. 1, a. 1, ad 7: "Voluntas numquam potest bene velle sine
divino instinctu; potest autem bene velle sine gratiae infusione, sed non
meritorie. Et similiter intellectus non potest sine *divino motu* veritatem
quamcumque cognoscere, potest autem sine *novi luminis* infusione, quamvis non ea quae naturalem cognitionem excedunt." ("The will can never
will well without the *divine instinct;* it can indeed will well, though not
meritoriously, without the infusion of grace. Likewise the intellect cannot
know any truth at all unless God moves it, but it can know without the
infusion of *new light*—though not things which exceed natural knowing
power.") It is quite clear from this text that *instinctus divinae* can mean
both actual grace and the general *motio divina* without which no creature
is active (in other words, creaturely activity remains borne up by God's
creation). In both cases, we have to do with one and the same divine, and
therefore creative, activity. But this is called *actual grace* if it is formally
a question of a divine *saving* (and also creative) activity.

offer with the (blind) dynamism of the human spirit and
thus ultimately interpret the old Christian idea of the beginning of faith (*initium fidei*) unbiblically. Thus he fails
to perceive that, in the process of development towards the
act of faith (*conversio*), the *instinctus fidei* is an inward instinct offering us in grace a *novum lumen* (it is an "instinct
bringing happiness") and at the same time prepares us, or
enables us freely to accept the offer (it is a *sufficiens inductivum*). To reduce this offer of grace to the *instinctus
naturae*—even if this nature is not viewed philosophically,
but theologically, and therefore as created by a God of
salvation—completely undermines the biblical message of
God's *agapē*.

Our human state is a constitutive but at the same time
powerless *need* for grace, and to such an extent that, without
grace, this humanity is personally meaningless.[44] Humanity
itself can, however, never be the *initium fidei,* and can never
of its own accord be a *de facto* offer of grace. It is only in the
warmth of God's saving love, to which (perhaps only implicit) consent has been given, that our humanity becomes
a grace. It is in this way that we become an offer of grace
for each other or the concrete form of the *initium fidei*
which through God's grace also feels its way in our fellow
men. We can, by virtue of God's saving will that is active
everywhere and in everything, escape this grace nowhere
(although we can refuse it). Wherever we turn, God's grace
is always there ahead of us. His face confronts us in everything. Is it, in that case, a bold affirmation to state that it
is not so very easy *not to believe* (even though a person may
casually assert that he does not believe)? Human weakness,
even human wickedness, is always weaker than the tri-

---

[44] Seckler struck a more fortunate note when he called this, correctly,
a "*pre*-evangelical climate" (and not the incipient evangelical climate of
the *initium fidei*).

umphant power of God's grace. I feel that this is undoubtedly Seckler's deepest intention, but why then does he say it in an explicit theology that identifies the miracle of grace with the cheerless limits of our finite nature, which can only be the hollow side of grace? And why does he only stress the fact that we find *ourselves* only in faith? That is, of course, certainly true, but is it not far more glorious to find in faith the wholly Other who places our life on an entirely different plane and is for us far more than simply an answer to the philosophical problem of our life?

Looking Forward from Aquinas's View

I should, however, not choose to look for the explicitation and extension of Aquinas's view of the light of faith and of the *instinctus fidei* (that is, the grace that invites us to believe) in the direction followed by Seckler, in other words, in the blind dynamism of the human spirit. I should prefer to look in a direction which, in keeping with Newman's "idea-impression," would provide a clearer analysis of how the so-called "ontological dimension" of faith (the light of faith) brings about a non-reflective, non-thematic and therefore confused *experience* in man (confused in the sense of being impossible to point out directly). To express this more precisely,[45] the inward divine invitation to believe is itself a (non-reflective) *experience* on man's side, an experience which, on reflection and in the light of the revelation in Word, can and must, however, be understood as coming from grace.

The problem of the meaning of the inward instinct of faith and of the external datum of faith can also be resolved

---

[45] I do not believe, as Seckler does, that the non-conscious aspect, or, as he calls it, the ontological aspect, has a greater ontic density than the psychological aspect.

in a less "formal" manner than in the theology of the Middle Ages with the help of a more refined anthropology. (By this I mean a study of man who come to himself in and through the world, finds himself only in the world and is therefore always bound to experience God's call in a human form that is intimately involved with this world.) Although it is clear that the full inspiring force of Aquinas's view of faith can only emerge as relevant for present-day reflection about the structure of the act of faith if it is divorced from the philosophy of *nature* with which it was so closely associated in Aquinas's synthesis, Seckler has nonetheless allowed the essence of this view to remain firmly within Aquinas's physical, "naturalist" framework.[46] The more obvious direction in which to seek the solution to this problem would be in that of the openness of the knowing and willing person who is confronted with a mystery which presents itself to him personally and to which he can only give his consent in the power of the living God. Yet Seckler[47] has attempted to find the solution in the direction of the blind dynamism of the spirit which permeates everything, including the intellect, and, penetrating to the intellect, arouses consciousness.

Philosophical analysis of our human experience reveals in man a positive openness to the Absolute, over which man, by definition, has no power—God must hold out his hand to man in grace, calling to him creatively to *come*. The *instinctus* in its original Greek meaning of *enthousiasmos* (with which Aquinas was familiar and which he quoted)

---

46 He has in fact embedded it even more deeply in this framework, by calling Aquinas's *desiderium naturale videndi Deum* a purely ontological, *blind* natural dynamism.

47 Perhaps inspired by J. Maréchal (whom he does not quote), possibly via the "action philosophy" of J. de Finance, *Etre et agir dans la philosophie de saint Thomas*, Paris 1943, which is mentioned in his bibliography, and therefore by M. Blondel.

might well have provided Seckler with a better indication of the direction in which he should have looked. "Enthusiasm" implies not only a being attracted, but also an *experience,* a state of being moved that is experienced in the person himself, but cannot of its own accord be explained by him because a deeper mystery is active within it.[48] Seckler places too low a value on the real aspect of experience that is present in the act of faith. In Seckler's view, grace becomes something rather like a non-conscious modality of human life (a typical affirmation of anti-Reformation theology), as though grace were a pure entitative elevation of our existence without our human psychology being affected by this process! There certainly is a non-conceptual element of experience in faith in Aquinas's *pre*-Reformation synthesis, even though this is embedded in his concepts and affirmations of faith (the *enuntiabilia*). Insofar, however, as there is an *experience* in faith, this experience does not refer directly to God's revelation of himself (this would be a *visio beata*), but to the value and the relevance of the truths of salvation to our human life. The experience refers to our human existence, to a certain state of *being moved* in this existence that cannot be explained from the human point of view, but that is experienced as a gift from elsewhere, a gift that, on reflection, can only be explained as a *grace*— the work of God's spirit in us.

Seckler too recognises that there is a non-conceptual element in the act of faith, but in his case this non-conceptual element is a blind unconsciousness, a not knowing—non-conceptual because it is not conscious. The author of this remarkable book has therefore, in this sense, missed a valu-

---

[48] See I, q. 87, a. 2, ad 1: "Fides . . . *percipitur* ab eo in quo est, *per interiorem actum cordis.*" ("Faith . . . is *perceived* by him in whom it is *through an interior act of the heart.*") Texts such as this have escaped Seckler's attention.

able opportunity. This is all the more regrettable because Seckler's teacher, Prof. J. Möller[49] (whom he does not, however, mention in his book) and Prof. M. Müller's book[50] (which is listed in his bibliography) could at least have helped to rectify, by means of the philosophy of Heidegger, his rigidly applicd philosophy of the dynamism of the spirit. He would indeed have found a clear warning—by overstatement in the opposite direction—against his identification of the revelation of being (*instinctus naturae*) and the inward revelation of salvation (*instinctus fidei*). Or is it simply that Seckler has ultimately only confused Heidegger's ontological *theio*-logy with theology proper? It is probable that this Heideggerian approach forms the background of Seckler's interpretation of Aquinas, but I cannot say this with any certainty. Very great concessions have certainly been made here to the demand for secularisation—indeed, they go too far for us still to believe in it. And I have not even raised the question of how reformed Christians will react to an invitation to believe that in no way differs from Aristotle's *naturalis appetitus boni!* It should, however, be borne in mind that these objections apply only to pp. 171–219 of Seckler's book, since the author's analysis of the structure of the act of faith according to Aquinas is undoubtedly the best that we have at present. Seckler has done even more than this—he has shown in this analysis how Aquinas, as a theologian, is still an inexhaustible source of inspiration for the solution of very modern problems. For Aquinas is indeed a source of inspiration, but not to those who choose to divorce themselves from the present-day experience of human existence and its analysis in modern philosophy and lock themselves up in a room with all of Aquinas's works.

---

[49] Möller's works include, for example, *Existenzialphilosophie und katholische Theologie*, Baden-Baden 1952.
[50] *Sein und Geist*, Tübingen 1940.

II

THE RENEWAL IN
PRESENT-DAY THEOLOGY

3 Salvation History as the Basis of Theology: *Theologia* or *Oikonomia?*

Introduction: Uneasiness in the Study of Theology

Students in all the living centres of professional theological activity have for years felt a certain dissatisfaction with speculative theology and even a resentment as far this branch of theology is concerned. This may, of course, be partly the fault of the scientific method as such. No science can be entirely free from the consequences of speculation, in which the person who is engaged in the study of any speculative science is bound to some extent to stand aloof from life if life itself is to be understood. All scientific study has to take this sense of annoyance into account, and I am sure that, unless he has indeed lost all contact with life itself, there is no speculative thinker living who has not, at some time or other, wished all his books in Jericho. This is, of course, a natural reaction on the part of anyone whose spiritual life is healthy, since reflection about life is certainly not life itself, even though it comes from life and in turn serves it. A theologian, for example, who devotes hours and days to the study of prayer, is bound occasionally to

79

recognise that the moment has come for him to stop specu-
lating about prayer and go and pray himself. Both activities
are necessary in the service of mature prayer.

However, this distance which every scientist must put
between himself and life cannot fully account for this disillusionment with theology; its real causes lie deeper. For
if the scientific method respects the essential structure of the
object of its reflection, it cannot lead to a total rupture
between life and thought. When such a gulf begins to open
up between the religious life or preaching, on one hand, and
theology, on the other, that we become aware of a complete
lack of continuity between the two, with each in effect covering a totally different field, we must then conclude that the
scientific character of theology can no longer be held responsible for this division; error must somehow have crept
into either the life of the spirit or theology and an alienation
from its original object must have taken place. For there is
no inherent necessity for reflection about the living content
of our Christian life—the reality of revelation which is at
the same time kerygma and the very content of revelation
that we experience as the crowning glory of our existence at
the level of our religious life—should produce resentment
and estrangement. Scientific reflection about what affects
us most intimately can hardly be anything but the extension
of the same interest at the level of speculative thought. A
cleavage between the two is something essentially abnormal;
its cause cannot be found in the essence either of the religious life or of scientific theology itself.

The solution cannot, of course, be found in something
extra—a sort of existential, affective dessert following an insufficiently nutritious theological main course. This would
lead to a twofold disillusionment, since no thinking person
can be satisfied by a few pious corollaries. The main dish

itself must provide substantial religious food, and it must do this for the thinking, speculative mind.

On the other hand, no solution is to be found in an effort to change the scientific character of theology, because any such attempt would simply mean leaving the vantage point of theology itself. The position taken up by certain kerygmatic theologians here is well known. These theologians were painfully aware of the fact that theology was no longer a preparation for preaching, that the content of faith as elaborated in the theology of the manuals and the same material as it had to be preached by priests to human beings were two totally different worlds. Not daring to attack the existing theology, these theologians set up beside it a kerygmatic theology in which faith and theology were closely connected. A theology was promulgated in which the consideration of everything *sub ratione Christi,* in the perspective of Christ, replaced the *ratio Deitatis,* God's own being—one which was not abstract and metaphysical but concretely concerned with the history of salvation. The *determinatio fidei,* the intelligibility of dogma, was given less consideration than its *Heilsbedeutung,* its saving value and meaning for life.

This theology of the history of salvation, especially that which follows the direction taken by Oscar Cullmann, has exerted a considerable appeal in recent years.[1] This Protestant theologian was violently opposed to any form of theology which was not based on the history of salvation; for he believed it to be infected by Greek thought, since the absolute norm of Christianity is historical, unlike the philosophical norm which is a transcendental datum situated outside history. "All Christian theology in its innermost essence is Biblical history; on a straight line of an ordinary process

[1] I am referring here to the years immediately following the Second World War.

in time God here reveals himself. . . . the self-revealing God, that is, his Word, his Logos, once entered so completely into history that this unique entrance can be designated by dates just as can every other historical event."[2] He regarded all history, even in its secular aspect, as belonging to one single and continuous line of Christ in which the *kairoi*— that is, the relevant moments of time, precisely selected by God as moments of divine and saving intervention—are, despite their diversity, in sharp distinction from each other and in irreplaceable originality. All these saving events are orientated towards one single fundamental *kairos*, the Incarnation of Christ's saving work, from which both the past and the future become intelligible in the present.

But this renewed interest was in fact associated with a complete depreciation of speculative thought. Moreover, by an astonishing short-circuit, it identified theological speculation with scholastic theology and, what is more, with the type of scholastic theology that was currently to be found in the theological manuals. All this was influenced and given momentum by contemporary existential thought, whose supreme expression was existentialism and in which pure conceptual thought—that is, the concept dissociated from experience—was rejected. In this way the value of conceptual thought as such was brought into question, including its value in theology. One would be blind if one failed to see that this anti-speculative tendency frivolously rejected, along with the parasite of pure conceptual speculation of later scholasticism, the best in the sphere of reflection about the faith that theology has acquired throughout the course of history. It would, of course, be wrong to try to minimise this failure to appreciate the deepest purpose of speculative theology by the facile explanation that this turning from

2 *Christ and Time*, rev. ed., Philadelphia, The Westminster Press, 1964, 23f.

conceptual towards historical and phenomenological thought is a purely modern and transitory phenomenon. We need not, after all, be particularly well-informed historically to know that the Church stubbornly resisted the introduction of philosophical conceptualism into theology in the thirteenth century—a well known example of this is the stand made in 1228 by Pope Gregory IX against the *philosophantes in S. Doctrina.*

The fact that seven hundred years later, in the encyclical *Humani Generis,* the Church reacted (correctly) against those theologians who were seeking to exclude conceptual thought from theology would at first sight seem to imply a contradiction within the Church, or else opportunism. Neither explanation, however, is the true one; for in neither instance was there a question purely and simply of a reaction on the part of traditional theology (which, in the first half of the thirteenth century, was still anti-speculative and, in the immediate past, speculative) against modernism—the medieval theologians, in other words, reacting against the modernism of the school of Albert and Thomas and the modern theologians reacting against the modernism of the anti-speculative, existential theologians. The problem is more complex and deeply rooted than this. What *is* indicated here is that while conceptual thought in all its forms is not pernicious, not every form of such thinking can be approved by the Church. There is, in other words, a rationalising kind of conceptualism which attempts to enclose the inexpressible in conceptual terms, and there is, on the other hand, a kind of conceptual thought which leaves the mystery *as a mystery* and tries somehow to express it precisely as a saving mystery, with the result that these concepts of faith radiate a value for life. The Catholic Church, then, has steadily opposed every devitalising conception of the dogmatic datum, and Aquinas's crowning

achievement in the sphere of theology may well be that he
built the value of dogma for life on the basis of its meaning and value as truth, while at the same time remaining
fully aware of the value of truth for human life.

Theology is, of course, a hazardous business, because the
theologian establishes himself completely in the reality of
revelation with the whole of his human spirit and thinking
mind. Theology is faith itself, alive in a thinking spirit.
This thinking on the part of the human spirit is never
finished. The growth of human consciousness is always continuing, and something new is gained in every age. But
every age without exception also has its own emotional and
theoretical emphases, which result in other affective and
intellectual aspects being thrust into the background. When,
for example, the incarnational tendency made its appearance
in the Middle Ages and Aristotle's *ratio* was placed in the
centre of *Sacra Doctrina,* this led not only to a great theological synthesis, but also to the conviction that the integrity
of human thought could only be protected by a religion
which was capable of philosophical thought. To live at the
same time from an authentic philosophy seemed to
strengthen authentic religion. Religion had to be able to
think clearly about itself, and philosophy seemed to be indispensable in this clarification, insofar as it was, for the
believer, the synthetic principle that connected his "openness to the world" with his "openness to God." Without
philosophy, theology would, it was felt, soon become diluted
to fideism and illuminism and be incapable of dealing with
contemporary problems.

But this emphasis on the use of philosophy in theology
is inevitably accompanied by the danger of one-sidedness,
the danger, in other words, that the aspect of mystery, the
basic resistance to complete intelligibility that is present
in the datum of revelation, may be forgotten. The con-

trary, however, is also true. In stressing this aspect of mystery and the saving significance of the reality of revelation, many modern theological movements also pay insufficient attention to the necessity of the *determinatio fidei,* the accurate definition of what enables the content of faith to be intelligibly understood within the mystery. This results in dogma becoming less clearly defined, and there is a serious threat that it may become emptied of content, or at least rootless.

The development of the synthesis between the tendency towards incarnation and the tendency towards disincarnation in theological thought will always be accompanied by painful conflicts. Harmony between nature and supernature, both at the level of human action and ascesis and at the level of theological thought, is not something that is automatically given, it is something that can only come about in a very laborious way. It is clear from the whole history of theology that reflection about the faith has in the end always followed the course of violent polemics and anathemas. In any renewal, what is authentic for Christian life is always mixed up with so much that is not authentic that the new aspects which again and again emerge must in the first place be purified. Every crisis is a crisis of growth, but what is taking form, throughout the course of time, in these constantly renewed birth pangs, is the sound growth of theology, which will continue as long as "we are away from the Lord" (2 Cor. v. 6). It would not be difficult to draw a historical curve, showing how secular culture—that is, the growth of human consciousness—has again and again sounded a new theological note. The grammatical tendency of learning in the Carlovingian period resulted in the grammatical element in the sphere of theology. Later, the discovery of dialectics led to the dialectical treatment of the datum of faith. The gradual introduction of Aristotle into the Western world gave rise to a speculative and philosophical theology. Positive theology came about as the result of the emergence of the historical method in secular learning. In the past, whenever a turning-point was reached, there was always a critical period of tentative searching until a balance was achieved. And this process is still going on—constantly developing human consciousness is even now always bringing new problems and new methods into prominence, and a period of crisis has to be passed through before a new balance is attained.

The study of history, then—which can provide us with a kind of sociology of theological thought—shows us that we may *a priori* expect every period to make its own *vox Dei* heard. It will also make it clear that we may also expect not only all *a priori* resistance to the new spirit of each period to be an attack against some new possibility in the sphere of theology, but also all *a priori* consent to the new notes sounded to be a possible source of danger to theology and to theological orthodoxy. The divine overtones that are present in each new sound can only be caught, the presence of the new spirit of each age can only be felt, and theology can consequently only be renewed and enriched, if we are deeply and lovingly anchored in the whole of tradition and if we at the same time submit to the guidance of the charismatic teaching authority of the Church.

We are therefore confronted today with the problem of choice between *theologia* and *oikonomia*, with the problem, in other words, of how theology should be practised—according to abstract metaphysical principles or along the lines of concrete saving history. Ought everything to be seen *sub ratione Christi,* in the perspective of Christ, or *sub ratione Dei,* in the perspective of God? Does the conceptual approach to the mystery of faith belong, in this context, to the past, and if we do not attempt to find more precise definitions, will this therefore lead to a sounder theology? Some

people are by nature speculative and others are anti-speculative, but temperament cannot be allowed to play a decisive
part here. It has, of course, nothing to do with this question,
even though, in certain cases, personal attitude may well
have an influence on the solution to the dilemma. We must,
on the contrary, let the objective structure of revelation
itself speak. If theology is nothing other than the scientific
status of the faith (*fides in statu scientiae*), the faith itself
as alive in the human, reflective spirit, then the very structure of the reality of revelation must show us objectively
whether we ought to follow a metaphysical, theocentric
course or whether we should proceed along the christological
lines of the history of salvation. The new note sounded by
the spirit of the present age will, insofar as it is authentic
and pure, be able to harmonise with the note sounded by
the ancient, traditional faith only if we in our own time
know how to listen correctly to the eternal symphony of
revelation. I shall therefore keep two aspects of the contemporary problem above all in mind in the exposition that
follows—the aspect of theology as characterised by the history of salvation and the conceptual character of theology,
both within the context of the christological focus of a
theology that is nonetheless essentially theocentric.

THE *THEOLOGIA* IS GIVEN TO US IN AN *OIKONOMIA*, A HISTORY OF SALVATION

The Historical Structure of Revelation within the Plan of Salvation

Aquinas formulated his point of view in the following way:
"In the most proper sense, theology provides ideas about
God as the highest cause, that is, not only insofar as he is
capable of being known from the created world, . . . but

also insofar as he alone knows himself and as he communicates this knowledge to others by revelation."[3] But the
whole problem is, what is the mode of this revelation? Is it
simply a question of a communication of a knowledge of
truths that are beyond our understanding, or is it primarily
a question of sacramental revelation, a revelation in human
and historical form? We should at the very outset be mis-
interpreting the data of the problem if we were to take the
assertion that Christianity involves revelation to mean that
God has revealed certain truths that are beyond our natural
understanding only as a kind of addition to an already acquired natural knowledge of God. It is, of course, certainly
true that the aspect of knowing in revelation is formal.
Revelation of necessity addresses a *consciousness*. But the
whole problem is, how does this revelation, this process
wherein the human consciousness is addressed by the living
God, take place concretely? We should not forget that the
dispensing and receiving of grace, the supernatural order
of life, by definition involves both salvation and history.
Through grace, God becomes a person for us—*Theos pros
hēmas,* the living God, as the Old Testament calls the God
of revelation.

The God of creation is, of course, also the personal God,
but he does not reveal himself in his creative concern with
the world as a person for us, thus enabling us to enter into
personal relationships with him. Personal relationships with
God are, of their very nature, of a theologal kind, even
though they are sometimes anonymously theologal. The act
of creation is certainly a free act on the part of the personal
God, but the true face of the living God does not emerge

---

3 See I, q. 1, a. 6: "Sacra autem doctrina propriissime determinat de
Deo secundum quod est altissima causea; quia non solum quantum ad illud
quod est per creaturas cognoscibile, . . . sed etiam quantum ad id quod
notum est sibi soli de seipso et aliis per revelationem communicatum."

from his creation. Creation does, however, offer us the possibility of affirming the personal character of God as a mystery, and this recognition forms the basis of the possibility of associating with God in grace. For, if at a certain point which is not grace, our human freedom were not able to come into contact in some way with the personal God, then grace or revelation would be impossible. It is precisely because grace is *grace,* God's free gift of himself, that it implies a *vis-à-vis* with the God of grace, a subject who can accept grace as grace, or refuse it—free man in the world, who is therefore, in a certain respect, not graced, although he is in some way already connected with God. It is, then, not the Aristotelian concept of "human nature" that makes us, as believers, distinguish between "nature" and "supernature," but the very essence of what grace is. It is this that implies the distinction between nature and supernature, even though the existential unity of nature and supernature must be established.

Creation does allow us therefore to affirm the personal God, but this personal character is not revealed in its personal life, its innermost aspect, in creation. In other words, the free activity of creation does not itself enter into human history, although it does constitute historical man. The activity of God's grace, on the other hand, is a free intervention on God's part in the history of man. This activity is itself historical, in the sense that God himself thereby enters into personal relationships with man in the (logically) already constituted history of man. It is, moreover, only the history of salvation that gives any intimation of the true face of the trinitarian God. Therefore, whereas God does not, by definition, enter as the creator into human history, which he transcends by being interior to it, the activity of his grace and revelation is, also by definition, certainly an intervention in human history, resulting in his commencing an existential dialogue with his people as man's partner, a dialogue in which he opens up his inner life to us. The whole history of the Old and New Testaments clearly shows us that man's life with his God is a historically connected, constantly developing dialogue between God and mankind. It is, then, the history of salavtion and not creation (which is, of course, the starting-point of the history of salvation) that reveals to us who God really is and his wish to be really our God, also for us men.

This revelation reached its culminating point in Christ. God entered into personal relationships with us in and through his humanity, of which the Logos is the person. A fellow man who treats us personally, then, is personally God. Jesus' human treatment of his fellow men is therefore an invitation to us to encounter God personally. Christ is the historically visible form of God's desire to confer grace and to do this in such a way that the gift of grace is essentially linked with something which is visible, a fundamental historical fact—the man Jesus. Grace therefore does not come to us directly from God's suprahistorical, transcendent will to love us, but from the man Christ Jesus. The gift and reception of grace, revelation, thus takes place within the framework of human intercommunication. Human contacts with the man Jesus, historically situated encounters, become, in other words, meetings with God, because it was God's plan to redeem us only in humanity. It is at the same time the perennial, lasting character of the mediation of grace through the man Jesus that demanded, from the moment of Jesus' pneumatic glorification, the introduction of the sacramental economy of salvation, the *sacramenta separata*. Social intercommunication between men, after all, takes place via physical nature. The glorified Lord therefore continues, as a man, to be the lasting instrument of salvation, and grace continues to be conferred within the terms of human intercommunication—between men and the man Jesus.

But, because the living Lord lives in a pneumatic (that is, spirit) situation which is therefore invisible to us and we, on the other hand, still live in an unglorified earthly situation bounded by time and space, the man Jesus, who is still living even now, is able to encounter and influence us directly, but is not able to make himself directly present to us *in propria carne*. The man Jesus still belongs to our earthly world, but at a point where this world is already glorified. As a result, then, a disproportion has arisen between us, as the unglorified world, and Christ, as the glorified world. It is only under sacramental symbols that God's eternally actual act of redemption performed in humanity can be made present to us in our earthly and historical world. Because of the perennial character of the man Jesus, as the only Mediator, "the same yesterday and today and for ever," the life of grace continues to take place, even after the closing of revelation, as a history of salvation, and our sacramental, historically situated encounter with the living Lord in the sacral sphere of Christ's Church is *the* encounter with the God of our salvation.

Throughout history, our only encounter with the *ratio Deitatis*, with God's own being, is in the man Jesus, in the saving history of the sacramental economy of salvation, in which God reveals himself personally, though in a veiled manner. This historical character of grace, or of the *agapē*, was clearly expressed by Paul in these words: "the love [*agapē*] of God in Christ Jesus our Lord" (Rom. viii. 39). It is not, then, directly a metaphysical divine quality, but it is this in a history—that is, in the man Jesus, God's act of love which enters human history and from which his essential, divine goodness emerges. The historical character of grace which brings about an *oikonomia* is a consequence of the fact that God, as a person taking an initiative, freely enters into dialogue with human freedom.

God's interior aspect—the *interiora Dei* of antiquity—is therefore communicated to us in a history of salvation, with the result that revelation is a saving event in which a divine reality in earthly, visible form touches the human reality. Revelation is not just the communication by speech of suprahuman knowledge by the prophets and ultimately by Christ. It is more fundamentally the historical accomplishment of a divine and suprahistorical saving initiative within the structure of human history, the significance of which, however, is disclosed to us only by the Word of God. Revelation is therefore a revelation both in reality and in word— in which, however, the word is essentially related to the reality that manifests itself. The two are indissolubly united. Revelation, then, is a *mystērion* in which we, listening in faith to the Word or the kerygma, penetrate the sacramental appearance to reach the divine *mysterium*.

In revelation, then, we certainly have to do with the "First Truth," as the medieval theologians called it, but with this truth as manifested in a saving history, or as Augustine expressed it, "the history of the realisation in time of God's providence,"[4] an economy of salvation as the sacramental appearance in time of the eternal trinitarian life of God. The trinitarian divine life—God's interior aspect—stands out against the background of a plan of salvation that takes place in time. Catholics therefore believe in earthly realities as tangible, visible and audible sacramental appearances of supernatural realities of salvation.

---

[4] See *De vera religione* c. 7 (*PL* 34, 128): "Historia dispensationis temporalis divinae providentiae."

The Consequences of This for the
Theological Method

This structure of revelation has precise consequences for the method of theological reflection. Aquinas correctly laid emphasis on the fact that the "revealed God"—God as God—is the subject of theology, but that we must also remain fully aware of how and where the divinity of God is revealed to us. It is in fact revealed to us in the inner light of faith, the objective content of which is given to us in the *theophaneia* of the history of salvation. Our knowledge of God, both natural and supernatural, is always analogous —we have no explicit intuition of God, no definition of God, but "we appeal in theology to the intelligibility of God's natural or supernatural effects, as the means of our knowledge of him."[5] It is a question of a knowledge "of the one through the other"—in other words, of one reality via another reality. Just as we know God humanly from his creatures, but in such a manner that we can never relinquish this bond with creatures and hence all our ideas of God remain creatural ("utimur effectu naturae"), so too, at the level of faith and theology, we know God only from the historical economy of salvation, and also in such a way that for our knowledge the history of salvation enters into the Christian definition of God himself ("utimur effectu gratiae"). It is therefore really a question of *theo-logia*, "God-learning," but of a *theologia* that is made known to us only in an *oikonomia*, a temporal plan of salvation.

To study a pure history of salvation is to neglect in principle the aspect of mystery proper to history, just as to

[5] See I, q. 1, a. 7, ad 1: "Utimur in S. Doctrina effectu Eius *vel* naturae *vel* gratiae, loco definitionis."

study pure theology is to disregard the fact that God revealed himself as God only in a historical plan of salvation or a saving event. The theologian who appeals directly to philosophical categories in an attempt to gain a deeper insight into faith, instead of appealing to the economy of salvation and devoting his attention to what salvation history can show us and enable us to experience, is turning his back on the real *epiphania Dei;* in practice, at least, he is claiming that the created world reveals the mystery of God to us better than does the history of salvation which God has brought about precisely in order to be able to show us his true face!

This insight into the structure of revelation shows us immediately that a theology based on the history of salvation cannot be opposed to a theology which accepts the divinity of God as the ultimate subject for consideration. Just as philosophy cannot speculate about God unless it proceeds from and remains constantly within the sphere of the created world, in which the aspect of divine transcendence is, as it were, seen, so too can theology have nothing to say about the God of salvation unless it too proceeds from and remains constantly within the sphere of the history of salvation, in which the God of redemption has revealed himself. If philosophy affirms that God is an absolute God, supratemporal, supraterrestrial and independent of the world, then theology also affirms that God is transcendent to the history of salvation. *Theologia* is therefore always based on *oikonomia,* but the two cannot be identified. We thus find the real object of the science of theology—God himself in his inner mystery—only at the level of the historically situated economy of salvation—that is, in the mystery of Christ. In theology, then, we certainly have ultimately to do with the intelligibility of God himself, but the history of salvation and therefore Christ is the only way towards this under-

standing of the *Deus salutaris*. And this is precisely the
meaning of revelation—that they should know the Father,
and Jesus Christ whom he has sent.[6]

It is therefore the concrete structure of revelation, as
briefly outlined here, that must define the theological
method. This structure shows us that we should not appeal
directly to philosophy—either Aristotelian or existential
(as Bultmann envisages)—in order to define the content of
revelation more precisely; in other words, for speculative
theology. Seen from our point of view, the history of salvation enters into the Christian definition of God ("Utimur
. . . effectu gratiae loco definitionis Dei"). The immediate
basis of our analogous knowledge of God is not the created
world and therefore philosophy, but the history of salvation, in which the created world is contained as an element
and as a substratum of the order of salvation.

An example may help to make this clear. A deeper
knowledge of the affirmation that God is Father and Son
and Spirit presupposes of course the human intelligibility
of natural fatherhood and sonship, but by referring to the
economy of salvation itself, to the reality which explicitates
the mystery of God—the reality of the appearance of Christ
as the medium through which the divine realities are revealed. The "visible mission of the Son" is the theologian's
real field of activity, the sphere in which he can more precisely define the deeper meaning of the divine Sonship.
Why, then, look immediately in the philosophical world of
creatures, if God reveals his true face in the history of salvation? I would almost say, why spend so much time scruti-
nising the *vestigium,* when the history of salvation can provide us with a clear *imago* of God himself which gives us a
far more direct view of the interior world of God? It is not

6 See John xvii. 3.

mere chance that the man Jesus is true God, yet was truly born as man (who was God). He was born, then, but still God—Son and God, and therefore God's Son.

This fact of the saving economy can provide us with a purer insight into the divine Sonship, and do this far better than a conceptual analysis of the human concept of "procreation." It is not as if the second Person is the Son of God only because of the economy of salvation. The very reverse is true—it is because he is the Son in the bosom of the Trinity that he, and not the first or the third Person, was born as man, so that his birth in time is for us the *locus theologicus,* the theological datum from which we can more precisely define the divine Sonship. This was furthermore the patristic method of proceeding, and it also still applies to the whole of theology, even to the *de Deo Uno,* or the "treatise on God." Why, then, appeal almost exclusively to the creatural perfections in order to define God's being more accurately, with the result that the theological treatise on God becomes a kind of reprint of the theodicy? "Do not even the Gentiles do the same?" God, after all, revealed his true face in the history of salvation and above all in Christ. How splendid and illuminating a treatise the *de Deo Uno* could be, if it were a theological reflection on the experiences of the people of Israel with their God in the history of salvation, which provides the clearest intimation of God's innermost being! The whole purpose of the history of salvation is to be an *epiphaneia* of God. The creatural perfections could then be included in this revelation, and thus be able to render valuable services.

The neglect of this view has been felt by those modern thinkers who are aware of the need for religious authenticity to be an estrangement from faith, because they feel, even though they are perhaps not yet able to formulate it clearly, that it is evident that the knowledge of what God really is and the understanding of what he really intends to be for us should be sought in revelation itself. We know that God is good from his creation, but the divine mode of this goodness emerges only from the history of salvation. "For God so loved the world," even though we cannot grasp the content of this divine mode in appropriate concepts. But when this goodness takes on the mode of the sacrifice of the Cross, when we see this goodness actively at work in the history of the stiff-necked Jews, then the light of the Christian goodness of our God dawns on us. If, however, we fail to take the history of salvation into account in our consideration of God, then we shall be turning our backs on the very reality in which God himself reveals and makes explicit the *interiora Dei,* his personal mystery, and looking for creatural analogies. And these are, after all, only a distant reflection of what is revealed to us in a more splendid and a more appropriate manner about God's holiness, justice, goodness, long-suffering and patience in the history of salvation.

When Aquinas spoke about "Christ who, as man, is for us the way leading to God" (I, q. 2, Prol.), he was at the same time stating, *ipso facto,* the theological method, since there can be no cleavage between life and reflection about the content of that life. This is an inevitable consequence of the objective character of our human knowledge. The manner of thinking may vary, but the structure of the content of faith remains the same.

We may therefore conclude that theology is essentially christological as to its method—in other words, that it has a basis of salvation history—but that it is theocentric and trinitarian so far as its proper object is concerned—a reflection about God who addresses us in an *oikonomia* or plan of salvation and whose speaking we hear only in the history of salvation. In other words, the way that leads to the inner mystery of God is the mystery of Christ, the history of salvation, which was commenced in the history of man, more sharply defined in the Old Covenant and completed in the historical Christ, and is encountered sacramentally and kerygmatically by us in and through the mystery of the Church. The economy of salvation must therefore always be the nursery bed of theology.

In this way, we have caught the divine note that sounds in certain contemporary movements, but we have at the same time made it harmonise with the older and well-known theocentric notes that no true theologian would ever neglect. In the history of salvation that cuts across human history, we always hear the *living* God, our God, the God of our salvation, God who, as God, is our salvation— "Deus qui sub ratione Deitatis est salus nostra." Revelation is an *appearing-making known* or a *making-known appearance* of a way of salvation, although not in an anthropocentric sense, since it is precisely in this "way of salvation" that God's name is revealed and glorified. That is why revelation is the hallowing or glorification of God's name in and through the faithful acceptance of this "way to salvation."

THE THEOLOGY OF SALVATION HISTORY AND THEOLOGICAL CONCEPTS

This brings us to the second question—is conceptual thinking and the appeal to philosophy excluded from theology by the foregoing affirmation?

Concretely, revelation is a history of salvation culminating in the incarnation of Christ and the mysteries of his life— God became personally a man and experienced his divine life in a human way. Now, in the life of a man, the human consciousness is the centre of the whole of his human activity. Christ's human self-consciousness is the consciousness of his own divinity—the incarnation of the divine consciousness in human psychology. The immediate source of what Jesus communicated to us in Holy Scripture is his human consciousness as illumined by his divine consciousness. In the one person of the God-man, then, divine knowledge is experienced in human consciousness and is therefore expressed in concepts, images and words which are derived from our world of human experience. The relationship between the concepts of faith and the reality of salvation eludes us—this relationship is, for us, a mystery. That these human concepts, which reveal the divine, do, however, in truth correspond to the divine reality of revelation is guaranteed by the mystery of Christ's appearance. As "totus in suis, totus in nostris," he was able to express, in a personal manner, the divine reality in suitable human images and concepts.

The economy of salvation, enacted in time and completed in the man Jesus, thus shows from the very beginning the direction in which the images and concepts of faith will move as expressions of man's contact with the saving reality itself. "The act of faith does not terminate in the concepts of faith, but in reality"[7]—the reality of salvation is attained in and through the concepts of faith by virtue of the light of faith as God's speaking inwardly and supernaturally to us. In this way, the concepts of faith are the reality of salvation itself, but, in that case, as known in faith by us men. The conceptual form to some extent expresses an implicit grasping in faith of the saving reality. The human process of bringing to awareness is simply not possible without some degree of conceptuality. Knowledge that is never expressed and therefore non-conceptual is not human consciousness, but an absence of consciousness—this is not pure

7 See II-II, q. 1, a. 2, ad 2: "Actus credentis non terminatur ad enuntiabile, sed ad rem."

theory, but a fact of human experience. Concepts belong essentially to the human process of bringing to awareness, but they can only grasp this saving reality insofar as they express the implicit grasp of the reality which is guaranteed by the "light of faith."

This expression in concepts is therefore the act by means of which the activity of knowing takes possession of a definite content of knowledge and appropriates it. The intimate "union of the spirit with God," to which Aquinas referred and which is given in and through the light of faith as the supernatural essence of faith, is thus connected with the concepts of faith, and these are included in the Christian consciousness. The inner light of faith or the *locutio interna* is attuned, and indeed exclusively attuned, to what the *locutio externa* or the history of salvation provides for us through the mediation of the Church, so to speak, from outside, and this always includes, as such, the use of concepts. The *determinatio fidei*, or our consciousness of definite contents of faith, is, as Aquinas stressed again and again, especially in his commentary on the *Sentences*, "from what is heard"—*fides ex auditu*. The real and the notional intellectual dimension of our faith are two inseparable aspects of our knowledge of the supernatural contents of faith. In this way, there is a definite element of conscious appropriation, of clarity and conceptuality, in the mystery of salvation as accepted by us in faith, and this element is expressed precisely in the concept of faith—in the *enuntiabile*. "Non enim posset homo assentire credendo aliquibus propositis, nisi ea aliqualiter intelligeret"[8]—there is no consent in faith without some understanding of faith. The concepts of faith thus point to the aspect of intelligibility that the subject can discover in the otherwise unfathomable mystery.

---

[8] II-II, q. 8, a. 8, ad 2.

Experience and concept, the light of faith and "faith from what is heard"—these always belong together.

The content of faith is therefore not a concept, but the God of salvation himself, adhered to in faith, really attained, not, it is true, grasped in concepts, but certainly aimed at in concepts. These concepts are the content of faith itself in its aspect of expression that is guaranteed by revelation.

It is here that certain kerygmatic theologians fall into error —by making a division between the definition of the content of faith and the saving value of this content, and by believing that the first should be neglected in favour of the second. We can, however, not reach the saving value of dogma unless we come to it in and through the saving truth of the objective reality of revelation, which must, as explicitly known, inevitably also be approached by concepts. Any dissociation of the *determinatio* or the content of truth from dogma as saving value will automatically result in pseudo-mysticism, pragmatism and subjectivism. The more purely, however, the significance of the content of revelation, as grasped intellectually in faith, is expressed in theological terms, the clearer and more meaningful will be the light that is thrown on the saving relevance of dogma. The intelligibility of dogma itself, the *credibile sub ratione veri,* must be the real point of light. The fact that this intelligibility can be expressed only in concepts is due to our human condition, which can become conscious of reality only by means of concepts. It is the fate of every science that aims at insight to make strict and severe demands on the human mind, and the science of theology is no exception. But anyone who thus possesses the content of faith in a scientific manner can penetrate so deeply to the heart of the mystery that he can fundamentally master the infinitely varied situations even outside the sphere of scientific theology—for example, in preaching—assuming, of course, that he has living contact with, and experience of, man as a concrete reality. He can do this precisely because his insight into the intelligibility of faith enables him to deal freely with dogma within the strict limits of orthodoxy. An autonomous kerygmatic theology, on the other hand, cut off from precise scientific definition, is, through lack of a precise *determinatio fidei*, from the very beginning limited in its varied manipulation of dogmatic preaching.

But speculative theology must also not lose sight of the distinctive nature of our conceptual knowledge of faith, and in this the historical Thomas differs quite radically from later Thomist thought, which was influenced by Scotism. The concepts of faith have a content that orientates us positively towards the reality of salvation—they contain an objective reference as knowledge, but they do not really grasp the reality in concepts. For example, the Fatherhood of the first Person is really situated in the objective perspective of our human concept "father," but we do not grasp conceptually the manner in which God's fatherhood is realised—all that we have as a conceptual content is the concept of human fatherhood. The fatherhood of God is certainly situated in the objective perspective of this human fatherhood, but we cannot locate it any more precisely within this perspective. We cannot measure the analogy. The concepts of faith are surrounded by human concepts which are, however, open to the mystery. The intellectual value of our concepts of faith is to be found in a projective act of knowing, through which we reach out in faith to God, without, however, grasping him conceptually, although we know that he is objectively to be found in the extension of, for example, our human concepts of father and son. In fact, we do not really apply the concept itself to God—the conceptual content rather tends towards God. God is therefore really Fa-

ther and Son, and it is not simply that we can only represent
him best in this way. We do not simply pretend that God is
Father—he is Father in himself. But we do not apply the
conceptual content of fatherhood to God—this only gives
us an objective orientation. Speculative theology is therefore
not in a position to conceptualise the mystery, but it can
preserve the objective perspective of the mystery from mis-
conceptions.

That is why, even in theology which is oriented towards
the history of salvation, metaphysics can and must have an
irreplaceable function to perform, although this is bound to
be subordinate.

Philosophy seeks the intelligibility of the datum of experience, and in this sense it is not dethroned by faith and
theology. Revelation itself does not provide us with any
supra-metaphysical truths, but only with explicitations along
the lines of salvation history. As a consequence, metaphysics
always has some contribution to make in any case in which
we have to do with the intelligibility of reality, even when
it is a saving reality. Although, in metaphysics, God is not
considered as God, but only as fundamental being, the divine being is nonetheless also a being and as such intelligible. It is certainly not a question of the mystery of God
being situated at a deeper level than the mystery of being.
It is one and the same mystery, reached metaphysically in
and through the created world and theologically in and
through the economy of salvation. Both views of God are
complementary to and throw light on each other. The existential unity between the order of creation and the order
of salvation is therefore the basis for the application of
philosophy in theology. In this sense, Pascal's distinction
between the "God of the philosophers" and the "God of
the history of salvation" is incorrect. Pure philosophy is
concerned with the Christian God, with the God of salva-

tion, insofar as he is attainable by means of natural human thought. But metaphysics does not come to God in himself precisely in this way, that is to say, it does not reach God precisely in his personal, dialogic relationship with man— it reaches in the creature *only* and *precisely* what must be assumed as a possibility for this personal dialogue if man is to be able to engage meaningfully in this dialogue. And it is precisely in this aspect that metaphysical insights can be put to the service of theological reflection about the manifestation of God in the history of salvation.

It is therefore clear that concepts, divorced from experience, are incapable of grasping reality and that a purely conceptual theology inevitably loses sight of its central point—that is, it becomes remote from the reality of revelation and eventually causes a cleavage between faith and theology. On the other hand, however, an anti-speculative attitude is also bound to lead to alienation from the specific content of the data of revelation, since theology is undoubtedly much more than history—it is salvation history. It is, then, basically a knowledge of historical saving events which are only the form in which the mystery of the saving will of the living God is made apparent. If we therefore maintain that the intelligibility of the living God, the *credibile ut intelligibile*, is the ultimate aim of theological reflection, then this also means that theology, however deeply embedded it may be in the history of salvation, will always result in speculative theology. If it does not, the human spirit, which is by nature attuned to intuitive knowledge, to a knowledge which strives to grasp being and is, in this sense, quidditative, will always be left dissatisfied. In this case, the dissatisfaction with theology that is felt today because of the continuing lack of a basis of salvation history would simply be replaced by another form of dissatisfaction —one already formulated by Thomas: "We must investigate the root of all truth ... establish the basis of this truth; otherwise ... we may know that something is as it is, but we shall have no real understanding and the spirit will remain, as it were, empty."[9] Both Augustine and Thomas even defined the act of faith as a restless and searching reflection based on firm consent: "cum assensione cogitare." Every reality, and *a fortiori* the divine reality of salvation, is, because of the transcendental character of the content of being, meaningful for living human thought and must be integrated in human life. Faith itself includes this aspect of reflection in inception, an aspect that, in theology, is only extended at the scientific level.

"I long to understand something of thy truth, my God, the truth that my heart believes and loves."[10] And we can say, together with Augustine, "Whoever believes, thinks [about his believing], and believing, reflects and reflecting, believes ... A faith that is not thought about is not faith."[11]

[9] *Quodl.* 4, q. 9, a. 3: "Debemus investigare . . . veritatis radicem, . . . scire quomodo sit verum quod dicitur; alioquin . . . certificabitur quidem quod ita est, sed nihil scientiae vel intellectus acquiret et vacuus abscedit."
[10] Anselm, *Proslogion,* Prooem.
[11] *De praedestinatione sanctorum* c. 5 (*PL* 44, 963).

4 The New Trends in Present-Day Dogmatic Theology

It is not my intention to provide an outline of what is happening today in dogmatic theology. I think it is preferable to indicate the new emotional and mental attitudes which are developing in this area. It should become clear from this sketch that the faith of thoughtful Christians—and hence dogmatic theology—living in the midst of an intellectual quickening and renewal, has undergone clarification. The meeting between new experiences, clarified by reflection, and the older insights into the faith has not only produced new problems in theology but has at the same time led to a fresh theological synthesis. For the new problems and insights have not simply been added onto the earlier theological findings in an external way, like an appendix. These older theological gains are themselves renewed by the modern problems and insights. For this reason, we are bound to say that not one single theological "treatise" or one part of such a treatise is excluded from the present-day theological renewal. (This is precisely why it is not possible to summarise the new acquisitions in dogmatic theology.) The truth contained in the older insights has, moreover, not been proved untrue in this process. It has rather survived in a higher entity. But in this new theological whole, the traditional insights have been purified and given new shades of meaning and even, here and there, basically corrected.

This process has taken place frequently throughout the history of the Church. It was strikingly evident, for example, in Aquinas's time. The older insights of the official theology of the Church that were current at that period—that is, Augustinian theology—were brought to life in a completely new way by Aquinas, who not only had a distinct feeling for the new Aristotelian, Arabian and Jewish philosophy that was coming to light in those days, but also went back to ancient scriptural and patristic sources. The elements of truth that had been acquired in the traditional theology were not sacrificed by Aquinas, but were rather incorporated in his synthesis as a result of a completely new presentation of theological problems. Very much the same thing is happening today. A complete renewal of dogmatic theology has been brought about in the thinking Church by the new perspectives opened up by modern thought, by a return to original sources, and especially to scriptural sources, and also by Catholic contact with Anglican, Protestant and Orthodox theology.

This gradual growth in knowledge of the faith is a consequence of the essentially historical nature of our existence. New aspects of the truth come to light only when the time is ripe for them; in other words, when man is able to take up that particular position from which a particular *as-pectus* of the reality that has so far not been seen becomes apparent to him. What is new in present-day theology should not therefore make us bewildered or suspicious. It is not a different theology that confronts us today, but the ancient theology of the Church that has come to possess the reality of the faith more firmly. It is, in essence at least, not purely a phenomenon of fashion. This renewal of theology is above all an opportunity for grace. At the same time, however, it can, now as at all times, also lead to the possibility of error. The harmony between "nature" and "supernature" is not, so to speak, automatically brought about in the incarnation of faith which has to be continuously renewed in human thought any more than it is automatically brought about in practical, active life. By definition this harmony can only be reached in detachment and constant self-criticism.

If the development of dogma and of theology is traced, it will be seen that one of the main factors in this growth, apart from man's constant return to the original sources in Scripture and Christian practice, is his vital awareness of the confrontation between the faith and new historical forces. Another principal factor, closely related to this, is the new trends of thought and opinion arising from human experience, which is constantly finding fresh expression, particularly in the literature and philosophy of an age.

We should not, however, forget, in connection with dogmatic development, that our faith in God never utters the first word in theological reflection. Religion and faith are a response—a reply—and therefore the second word. The first word is spoken by God himself. The whole basis of our concrete religion is revelation, and revelation is that extremely personal divine gesture through which the living God as it were steps outside himself and approaches us with the offer of his love—the offer of "communion with him," of a love which is fulfilled only when we return it. It is through this personal relationship with God—a son's relationship with the Father, the relationship of a son who, in Christ, grows to the full stature of a mature man—that we come to live in the grace that makes us holy. Our fumbling expression of this situation is that we *have* sanctifying grace. In reality, it is far more than this—we are taken up into a living communion with God, we live, have our being, and move in the rhythm of the divine life. We dwell in God, as in our own house. Quite individual, personal relationships exist between God and ourselves.[1] Drawn by this divine offer of love, which we can only accept in faith, and hoping and trusting that this initiative in love will, in the future, take personal care of our lives, we too, by virtue of the divine love that is given to us in Christ in the boundless infusion of his Holy Spirit, step outside ourselves into this communion of love.

In its essence, then, the content of faith, or revelation, is an invitation to salvation made by God to living mankind, a giving of himself on God's part. The word of revelation is directed, through the medium of the history of salvation, to the whole of mankind, and inwardly to the heart of every man. It is also addressed to us. What is heard must therefore always be brought into close association with the contemporary spiritual situation of the men who here and now hear God's Word. For this reason, the exegete has to attempt to establish how the Word of God was spoken to and heard by Israel, the apostles and the early Church. The dogmatic theologian, on the other hand, tries to establish how the same Word—heard by Israel and the apostolic Church and nonetheless also directly addressed to us, men of the twentieth century, in and through the actual grace of

---

[1] The *religious* relationship between God and man on the basis of sanctifying grace can therefore not be expressed in terms of relationships of "cause and effect." It transcends such relationships. On the other hand, however, this living communion with God does not fall outside God's universal causality, because even God's action "outside himself" is divine—it is an absolute activity and thus "creates from nothing." This explains the necessity of the *gratia creata*, created grace, as an ontological implication of the reciprocity in grace between God and ourselves. The mere "phenomenology" of the "encounter" cannot account for this.

faith—should be heard in its pure form by us now. How God spoke to Israel and how he spoke, in Christ, to the early Church, and how Israel and the early Church understood and experienced this Word must, of course, already have been determined before this work is undertaken. There can, therefore, be no dogmatic theology without exegesis and biblical theology. The hearing of the word of God by Israel and the apostolic Church forms part of the constitutive phase of revelation and is therefore *ephapax*, a unique and unrepeatable event, which will always act as a norm to the obedient listening of the post-apostolic Church. But, on the other hand, although revelation continues to be closed, God still speaks to us here and now in and through the "light of faith." This is indeed so true that the contemporary mode of our listening to God's word does to some extent come within revelation, as is clearly disclosed in any so-called new definition of dogma. When, for example, the Council of Chalcedon expressed the saving reality that is Christ in the affirmation "two natures, one person," it heard the same in this affirmation that the apostles had heard from their experience of the reality of Christ, and yet the manner of appropriating this same Word of God is different. This appropriation, however, not only belongs to the dogma, it is the dogma itself.

However absolute and unchangeable the saving value may be, it nonetheless shares, as something that is known by us in faith, in those characteristics which are distinctively human—in the imperfection, the relativity and the growth or historical nature of every human possession of truth. We must always distinguish, in the implicit totality of faith, between the reality of salvation and our consciousness of this reality in explicit faith at any given moment. It is a consequence of our physical nature and our situation in this world, without which the life of faith is not possible,

that our awareness of faith is always a vision of the reality
of salvation, seen in a certain perspective. Every human affirmation of faith is therefore open to growth and to amplification from the implicit totality of faith. We are never
able to make any definitive and all-round statements concerning faith. Our faith, which is manifested in an earthly
and human form, provides us, from a finite, limited and
historical standpoint, with a view in perspective of the absolute reality of salvation which we, because of our very
nature, never have in our power—not even in the beatific
vision of God. The saving value does not change. Even our
concepts of faith do not change. What does change is the
perspective within which we view the saving reality via our
concepts (which naturally include images). This perspective
varies throughout the course of history and from person to
person, thus bringing about the *growth* of our possession
of the truth or of our personal faith and of our concepts of
faith. It is via diverse and constantly changing perspectives
that we come ever closer to a better understanding of the
absolute reality of salvation. It is sufficiently clear from our
thorough *consciousness* of the fact that we always view the
saving reality in a changing perspective that we do certainly
encounter it in its absolute character, since this means that
we at the same time rise above the perspective and transcend
the relative in our vision.

This, of course, emerges clearly from Scripture itself. It
is quite possible and permissible for us to speak—correctly
—of a synoptic, a Johannine and a Pauline image of Christ.
We are unmistakably faced with three very divergent views,
which do, however, come into contact "somewhere" with
each other and are complementary to each other. To make
an absolute of, for example, the synoptic perspective would
eventually lead to Nestorianism, whereas to give an absolute
value to the Johannine vision would, on the other hand,

lead to a denial of the full consequences of the true and
developing manhood of Jesus. This is precisely why every
form of conceptualism—and by this I mean, in this context,
the giving of an absolute value to one vision of Christ expressed in concepts—is, by definition, the most extreme
relativism, because it makes absolute one special perspec-
tivist view of the absolute and thereby excludes any complementary vision. This relativism is all the more dangerous
because it presents itself under the cloak of synoptic or
Johannine orthodoxy.

Every period of history, then, is characterised by its own
special points of view. Man is made most clearly aware of
these new points of view in philosophy (and, in a distinctive way, in literature). That is why, throughout the history
of the Church, every new development in theological
thought can be seen to have been closely associated with
a development in universal human thinking. In this way,
philosophy especially has continued to present theology
with one chance after another of deepening its insight into
the reality of revelation. But, although contemporary philosophy does compel the Christian thinker to trace the connection between the word of God and the spiritual situation
of his time, it is at the same time clear that errors in this
new philosophical thought also cause frequent conscious or
unconscious "heresies."

Here I propose to discuss only a few of the most striking
features of this new human awareness and to consider its
repercussions on dogmatic theology. In this, I shall not aim
at providing a complete picture and shall deliberately even
omit certain problems because a discussion of these would
require a separate exposition. Among such problems are
those which really belong to a general "introduction" to
theology—questions, for example, of "tradition," "religious
projection," "demythologisation" and so on.

THE APPEAL TO HUMAN EXISTENTIAL
EXPERIENCE

Theology is the faith of the thinking man—it is a reflection about faith. For this reason, every believer is virtually a "theologian"—as a man, he thinks about his being a believer. In many cases, this is not done methodically, but happens spontaneously at certain occasions, especially as a result of practical experiences of life. But this reflection can also take place systematically, methodically and scientifically, in which case we speak of theology as a science, although it is a science of a very special kind. Not every man is called to practise this science, just as not every man is called to be a doctor, although every man is indeed called to have some knowledge of the practical care of his health. The scientific examination of human experience employs a different method of working from the spontaneous examination. On the other hand, the call to practise the science of theology is by no means confined exclusively to priests. Indeed, it is even questionable whether the ordinary priest in the parish, engaged in pastoral work, is really called to practise theology *as a science*. It is, of course, true that he is bound to study the totality of faith in a more methodical and systematic way, but training for the priesthood is, in fact, not an education for the practice of theology as a science. This is always a personal vocation, which is addressed to laymen as well as to priests. It is an established fact that in the first centuries of the Church's history the science of theology was to a very great extent in the hands of laymen and of bishops, and only exceptionally in the hands of priests. But even if theology is regarded as a scientific reflection about faith, this specialised activity cannot be divorced from the believing community. In a certain sense, we may say that theology as a science is a reflection deriving from the entire community of believers and expressed through the mouths of the theologians. This theology issues from faith and flows back towards faith. It serves as a mediator between the simple faith which is largely "anonymous," with its spontaneous expression, and the faith which is more explicit and thus stronger and more personal.

Faith and reflection about faith are, however, two completely different orientations of the spirit. Although faith is an "existential act," theology as a science is not. As reflection, theology is an act which, *as such*, stands outside man's affective and practical attitude towards the reality of faith. Although it does come within the sphere of living faith, it nonetheless preserves a certain "distance" from life, partly so as to stress the orientation of religious practice towards reality. "Life" and "thinking about life" do constitute a single whole, because human life is not simply lived but is of its very nature a life that man himself must direct; yet there is a difference between the two within this one totality of life. The point of rest at which the searching mind takes a certain distance from life, precisely in order to fathom its meaning and to be able ultimately to give it a true direction, does not correspond exactly with lived life.

It is from this difference between life and reflection about life, within the distinctive character of the human sphere of life—man's life is, of its very nature, a life which thinks about itself—that one of the basic attitudes of theology as a science becomes clear. This is that the science of theology never separates the saving value from the value as truth. It is precisely in the saving truth that the theologian discovers the saving value of revelation for man. It is only if it is directed towards that—that is, if it recognises the value of *truth* itself for life—that theology is able to nourish the life of faith. Theology is concerned with the reality of faith, which is meaningful for man precisely in its absolute character. This act of theological reflection does, it is true, come from life and it does serve life, but as such it is a reflection about life. It is here, then, that the real testimony is to be found. This testimony is not the same as that of preaching or the kerygma, but it has its own special place in the fullness of the life of the Church and ultimately serves the Church's subsequent preaching by its distinctly scientific character.

1. Theology is a reflection about the mystery of faith and, in the light of this mystery, about problems of life in this world. This *mystery*—the revelation in reality itself, with which we come personally into contact through the "light of faith"—is clarified by the prophetic word (and ultimately by the prophetic office of the Church) in the *concepts* of faith, the expression of which—dogma—is, so to speak, the exponent. The reality of salvation, the concepts and images of faith and their expression constitute one single, undivided whole.

An important insight in this connection is that this divine mystery, the very centre of theological speculation, is not a supra-mystery with regard to the mystery which man's spontaneous or reflective and philosophical thought encounters. We are, in faith, not concerned with an "analogy in the second power." The mystery of faith is rather a disclosure of the same divine mystery which shows itself at the end of human thought. The consequence of this is that the revelation of this mystery takes place in and through saving facts—it is not a revelation, as it were, of a new kind of metaphysics, a kind of supra-metaphysics. The life of grace implies that, at a point which is not yet grace, man already has a certain contact with the divine mystery. The result of this, as far as man situated in history is concerned, is that when God, in his grace, wishes to come into personal contact with man, this contact, or revelation, itself makes history. Revelation is accomplished in a history of salvation; that is, in the history of mankind which God confronts not only as the Creator who transcends everything by being interior to it but also as a partner in life who enters human history by drawing near to meet man, and who thereby really makes this history into saving history, while leaving its strictly historical character intact.

Man's experience of the life of grace on earth is therefore existentially quite different from his experience of glorification in heaven. The believer is related to God, on the one hand, by the grace of faith, hope and love, through which he possesses a supernatural, personal orientation towards God; but, on the other hand, he is characterised in all his living actions as well as in his faith, hope and love by his physical nature within this world. It is only when the beatific vision is made incarnate in our pneumatic physical nature, it is only when we are made entitatively supernatural even in our physical nature, that we can speak of a real experience of God, for it is only then that we are completely the subjects of a supernatural experience of reality.

Here on earth, a personal contact with the living God that is already present in faith can certainly refashion our deepest mode of being, our actions and our insights, but this mode of being, this attitude to life and these insights can only be realised in the natural form of our humanity. That is why revelation does not come to us in heavenly concepts and words, but in concepts and words, images, actions and signs that are rooted in our natural existential experience. When we name God, to whom we are personally oriented only in faith, we give him names which are derived from our experiences here on earth, and which are ultimately derived from Christ's consciousness of himself, that he expressed in words, concepts and images derived from his own human existential experience. The distinctive character of man's natural existential experience is therefore fully maintained, but it is at the same time incorporated in a supernatural orientation towards God, which imparts to all our actions a content that cannot always be expressed explicitly, but that certainly breaks through in Christian life and experience. "Your life is hid with Christ in God. When Christ who is our life appears, then you will also appear with him in glory" (Col. iii. 3–4).

This not only lays stress on the essentially eschatological orientation of our life of grace on earth. It also makes it quite clear that the supernatural quality of this life is still concealed. The full and explicit experience of the supernatural quality of our life takes place only in the beatific vision of God, embodied in our pneumatic physical nature. Here on earth we live, in the fullest sense of the word, in and from the mystery. Any theology which disregards this is only turning the whole of man's life of grace on earth upside down, forgetting that here on earth our life is not yet revealed. The life of grace appears only in the form of natural physical being within this world, with all its consequences.

2. This earthly structure of our personal communion with God determines the method employed by dogmatic theology. The content of faith, which is, in its distinctive quality, really inexpressible here on earth, is expressed in concepts which are rooted in a certain experience—in our experience of the history of salvation. But it follows from what I have already said that there is, parallel to and within our personal but veiled involvement with the reality of divine revelation (thanks to the grace of the light of faith), a reference in our so-called concepts of faith to our natural existential experience, and thus to the natural light that is contained

in this experience and makes it meaningful, the source of many insights which, in union with our experience of faith, express something of the reality of salvation.

If, for example, the Christian concept of divine providence is not an empty word for us, it presupposes a two-fold experience and reflection about these experiences. First of all, it assumes that we have had experience, in our lives, of the watchful care of a loving being—a father, mother or friend. Without this worldly experience of providence, the word and concept "providence," as applied to God, would have no meaning for us. It is only on the basis of this content and meaning that we can, without being able to form any real idea of it, really aim at God's providence. Secondly, it assumes that man can by his natural powers arrive at some idea of God. Without this basis of a natural reaching out to the Absolute—of whom we cannot take possession but who, on the contrary, demands our complete surrender to him—the Christian faith would be devoid of intelligibility and the projection of our worldly idea of providence onto God would have no objective value. It would be a purely "religious projection," made not from an objective dynamism of the reality, but by a subjective projection without any *definite* direction and without content and meaning—in a word, empty.

This single example should show how closely speculative theology must seek to associate itself with human existential experience. The human idea of providence, for example, points to an experience which belongs to the order of fellowship; it is a specific form of intersubjectivity, of mutual presence and dialogue. From this concrete experience, we then analyse the constitutive elements of this worldly providence in the order of a phenomenology of encounter, and from this we can open a certain perspective onto divine providence. This openness, this perspective whose horizon is lost to our view, arouses a certain longing and expectation in us. It points to a further possibility—that of a free, personal God. Then we see how this possibility, which was prepared in the Old Testament, was realised in the man Jesus. We see how God's concrete providence and care is really present in Christ, how it is *shown*, *realised* and in addition *resolved* in Christ. In this way, we keep in constant touch, in theological reflection, with the concrete reality; that is, with human existential experience and with the history of salvation, in which the living God allowed Israel and the man Jesus, and still allows his Church, meaningfully and actively to experience the reality of salvation. We do not by reflection lose contact with reality and with experience—we do not even lose touch with personal experience of life, since God extends his personal gesture of salvation to the history of every human being.

In my opinion, then, one of the most striking characteristics of the new theology is that a conceptual element is essentially present in human thought, but that human thought is not nourished by concepts, but by experience— by varying perceptive contacts with the reality of salvation. Later scholastic theology especially, and in particular the theology of the Enlightenment, of which our present-day theological manuals are the inheritance, tended to regard experience simply as a point of departure providing concepts, in the view that all further thought could take place purely conceptually. The phenomenological, existentialist tendency of recent dogmatic reflection is, on the other hand, in striking contrast to the "essentialist" theology of the past.

It is, however, true to say that, in certain theological movements, those who follow this modern tendency do go to extremes by setting their face firmly against all conceptuality and practising a literary and phenomenological kind of theology which really has nothing in common with theology proper. These modern theologians seem to forget that any phenomenological elucidation of faith will be quite inadequate if it fails to penetrate to the metaphysical implications of the life of faith and if it neglects the distinctively divine manner of, for example, the reciprocal relationship between God and man. Furthermore, they also seem to forget, in fact, though not in theory, that conceptual theological knowledge is really the expression *par excellence* in this world of the content of man's experience of faith.

The playing with concepts which characterised later scholasticism has nowadays frequently been replaced by a kind of literary playing with phenomenological ideas on the part of those theologians who claim that they are orientated towards phenomenology. And this tendency constantly brings the authentic theological renewal into disrepute. Confronted with such phenomenological attempts to reach an understanding of the dogma of the Transubstantiation, for example, we are forced to admit that these studies provide an excellent *introduction* to the theology of the Transubstantiation. But they do not come anywhere near the real problem of the dogma. In the belief that they are interpreting the dogma in a modern theological way, all that these theologians have in fact succeeded in doing is unwittingly to coat the dogma with phenomenology. In reacting—rightly—against a form of metaphysics that was cosmologically orientated, their mistake has been to abandon metaphysics entirely in their phenomenological analyses and to forget that it is possible to renew metaphysics on an anthropological basis. On the other hand, scholastic reactions to phenomenological analyses of this kind manifest such a physical approach and such a lack of understanding of phenomenology that even these speculations about the Transubstantiation fail to satisfy us and can therefore only save it verbally.

I am of the opinion that a state of balance has by no means as yet been achieved in this eager recourse to phenomenological analyses, however necessary these may be in theological renewal. It is here, I believe, that the critical point of the new theology can be found—the point at which theology will either go on to make a new, authentic flight or else be fatally grounded in a complete emptying of content of the Catholic faith. This danger is, in my view, very real today. Its chief exponent is H. Duméry, despite the many splendid pages that he has been able to offer us.

In the foregoing remarks, then, I have attempted, by assuming what is to follow, to show in a few words the inevitably earthly form of theological thought. This form contains the reason for the continuous renewal of theology. An appeal to the constantly growing elucidation of human existential experience is a matter of life or death for genuine theology.

THE ANTHROPOLOGICAL IDEA OF INCARNATION: GREATER AWARENESS OF THE "HUMAN CONDITION"

Recognition of the Distinctive Character of the "Human Condition": Its Good Influence on Dogmatic Theology

Probably the most important advance made by the philosophy of modern phenomenology is its recognition of the distinctive character of the "human condition" and its resolute abandonment of physicism, according to which man, like the things of nature, was seen as something that is "determined by nature." The distinctive, anthropological character of man, whose mode of being and mode of being one is to be found in an essential correlation between the spirit which communicates itself to the body and the physical nature which participates in this spirit, is nowadays becoming increasingly clear. This insight could be called the affirmation of man's essential incarnation, in which man is also seen as a fundamental freedom, and as a "possibility" (*Wesen der Moglichkeit*). For the first time in history since the Hellenistic period, we are confronted by a complete break with the dualist conception of man. A synthesis between the consistent acceptance of personalism and the recognition of the essential incarnation of the human person is gradually coming about. This has enabled us to see more clearly than in the past that the specifically human character of man is not something that is given, a datum, but a task, something that has to be realised (and therefore also something that can be neglected!). But it has also enabled us to see, on the one hand, that man is spiritual even in his physical nature and, on the other, that all his activities, even his most exalted spiritual and religious actions, always bear the stamp of his earthly physical nature. It is only in this world that man comes to himself. He impresses the things that surround him with the stamp of his humanity and it is only in this way that he can live as a man, even insofar as he is religious. All this places greater emphasis both on human freedom and on the situational character of this freedom and at the same time enables us to gain a more subtle insight into the essential ambiguity of everything that is human.

The basic insight in all this is that we have learned to realise more clearly (although this is not always seen uniformly and is also often seen to the detriment of the human spirit) that human consciousness is an incarnate consciousness. In other words, it enters the world by means of the very act through which it constitutes itself, that is, by communicating itself to that piece of worldly reality that is our own biologically sensitive physical nature. In a word, it is a refinement of the ancient affirmation, *anima est forma corporis.*

This recognition of the "human condition" has caused "revolutions" in the sphere of dogmatic theology, or, more precisely, it is in the process of causing them—in christology and mariology, in the study of the Church and her sacraments, in eschatology and even in the doctrine of grace and in treatises on faith, hope and love. I can do no more than provide a broad outline of a few of these.

The mystery of Christ and the Trinity.[2] The more finely shaded insights of modern anthropology have also permitted a purer dogmatic light to be thrown on the implicit riches of Christ's "true humanity." In this, the antitheses between the Alexandrian and the Antiochian christologies, which have persisted throughout the entire history of the Church, have gradually been overcome. The affirmation that Christ is not a human person *besides* being a divine person has undoubtedly been preserved (although sufficient justice has not always been done to this affirmation in certain circles). On the other hand, the humanity of Christ has not been "depersonalised"—a thing that occurred quite frequently in some theological manuals, which referred in so many words to the "impersonal human nature" of Jesus. Jesus' humanity is thus seen as personal, although not as a "human person." Jesus' humanity is regarded, in a more consistent way, as the basis, not indeed of his state of being a person, but of his state of being a person in a human manner. The Son himself is personally man, and the man Jesus is personally God the Son. A human act on Jesus' part is therefore a personal act of God appearing in human form. The entire concrete existence of this man is thus a grace,

[2] In view of the fact that I am only giving a few guidelines here, this christological outline will inevitably be very concise and schematic.

because this man's state of being a person for this humanity, which does not belong to itself but to the divine Son, is pure grace.

Since the Son is moreover only a person in his antithetic relationship with the Father and the Son's state of being a person consequently does not include but essentially is a subsisting I-thou relationship with the Father and the Holy Spirit, Christ too is only a person insofar as he is, by means of the hypostatic union, in an essential, personal relationship with the Father and with the Holy Spirit.

This ontological situation has its inevitable repercussion on Christ's human consciousness of himself. The "ontological person" must totally embrace the "psychological person" in itself, and this only means that a person is a being that is in itself and is therefore "illumined" from within. If true humanity is, then, impossible without consciousness of self, this means that Jesus' human consciousness, which, like his humanity, is of its very nature a *grace*, implies an intuitive human experience of his divine self, insofar as this self is conscious of itself in a *human* consciousness. In this perspective, light is thrown on what was elaborated for the first time in Latin theology by Aquinas as Christ's "experimental knowledge" in its distinctively human aspect, and it becomes at the same time apparent that there is nonetheless a certain distinction between Christ's viatorial *visio immediata* here on earth and his *visio beata* in heaven. The consequence of this consciousness of himself on the part of the man Jesus because of his essential relationship with the Father is that the Father is the centre of Christ's human consciousness. And if all speaking on the part of one man to his fellow man is a revelation of himself, this means, as far as Christ is concerned, that all his human speaking and all his human activity is, by definition, a revelation of the Father and a pouring out of the Pneuma.

This is bound to make us even more explicitly aware of the fact that Christ's incarnation was a *becoming* man, a growing reality. It was not something that took place at one moment, for example, at the moment of conception in Mary's womb. His incarnation, his becoming man, was a growing reality which continued throughout the whole of Jesus' human life and which found its active point of rest in the closing aspect of the incarnation—Jesus' resurrection, glorification and eschatological pouring out of the Spirit.

Acceptance of the personal character of the incarnation has also made us all the more clearly aware of Christ, not only as the revelation to us of God's invitation of love, but also as the person who, as a man, accepted this offer of love from the Father. For this reason, we are bound to say that divine revelation was accomplished in and through the religious life of the man Jesus. His personal relationship with the Father in confrontation with the world was the source of Jesus' discourse addressed to his fellow men, in which he revealed the concrete form of all true religion to us. Religion itself is the sphere of revelation, which is therefore essentially a dialogue.

This more finely shaded insight into the personal mystery of the man Jesus has also resulted in Christ's *kenōsis* occupying a central position in present-day dogmatic theology. According to a phrase in Paul's letter to the Philippians— "he emptied himself" (Phil. ii. 7)—what the incarnation meant for the human experience of the Person of the Son was a *kenōsis* of self-emptying. Dimensions of which Christians were far less aware in the past have been discovered in this "human condition" of Christ. Until recently, with the exception of Ambrose, theologians—at least all those of the Latin tradition—tended to regard this *kenōsis* as of minimal importance and applied it only to Christ's suffering and death. Now, however, it is seen to be of the greatest importance, something that embraces the whole of Jesus' human life as a "situated human freedom," sin excepted. The *kenōsis* is thus seen to permeate Jesus' entire situational existence, and this view has led to the insight that Jesus, although personally God the Son, could, as a man here on earth, only be a conscious being in a human manner.

This movement has also led to the disclosure of more profound perspectives in the treatise concerning the "mysteries of the life of Christ" (*mysteria carnis Christi*) and consequently in the doctrine of the redemption. The biblical insights, according to which there is a reference in the idea of the Fatherhood and the Sonship to the *risen* Christ and to the pouring out of the Holy Spirit (by means of which we come to share in this resurrection, Rom. viii. 15–17), are very closely associated with the modern anthropological view. The biblical doctrine of the redemption has thereby acquired greater dimensions and the resurrection has once again been accorded a central place in this doctrine. In speculative christology, this has at the same time brought the treatise on the Trinity into far closer touch with the mystery of Christ, and, via the christological mystery, the treatise on the Trinity has thus also been "renewed." Moreover, purification of the physicist concept of "nature" has provided us with a better understanding of the divine nature. We no longer see this as a kind of communal, neutrally divine background to the three divine persons, but as indicating the manner in which these persons are one, as pointing to their community or *perichoresis*. Greater significance has also been given to the trinitarian character of the incarnation and of the redemption, and the treatise on God (the *De Deo uno*) has become from the very outset a theological treatise on the Trinity (although there is a tendency nowadays to avoid the word "treatise").

The fact that the person is no longer regarded as extrinsic

to "nature," but nature as the content of the person has also had its repercussions on the classic doctrine of the *instrumentum coniunctum*, by which patristic and scholastic theology tried to justify the saving value of Jesus' human actions. The sacramental saving manifestation of Christ is thus more closely related to his personal activity than it was in the case of the theory of the *natura humana ut instrumentum*, and has thereby acquired greater religious depth. In addition, the idea of the "intersubjectivity" between ourselves and the man Jesus, who is personally God, has made it possible for the doctrine of grace to be expressed more in existential terms than in predicamental concepts.

The Church's teaching on the subject of Mary has also been purified by the new insight into the fully human condition of Jesus' life. In certain mariological tendencies in the past, Mary was to some extent obliged to make up for the deficiency that was believed to exist in Jesus' humanity.

It is perhaps characteristic that the whole of this speculative "renewal"[3] due to anthropological insights is accompanied by a differently orientated historical judgment of, for example, the christology of Theodore of Mopsuestia, which in the past was always regarded as suspect. In spite of some awkward formulations, this teaching now appears to those who support the new historical research as orthodox and Catholic. These parallel influences can, in my opinion, be explained by the fact that the content and meaning of the past—of the Bible and of patristic theology, for example—become constantly clearer according to the light in which these writings come to stand in the continuously renewed spiritual situation of mankind. Historical research in the sphere of exegesis must go on all the time, since

---

[3] Once again, I must stress that this "renewal" should be seen as a throwing of new light on what was previously latent and unexpressed, but nonetheless implicitly accepted.

the past is never completely dead for man. The content of the Bible speaks to us even now, not only in the light of the word of revelation, but also in the light of our present-day awarenesses, perspectives and insights. For this reason, we are right to refer to a biblical theology as a part of dogmatic theology, a biblical theology in which the light of faith includes within itself the light of the intellect, that is, the light of human experience that reflects about itself. We therefore recognise that in each period of history man approaches Scripture differently and thereby discovers aspects which escaped the attention of those who studied the same Scripture in previous periods. This certainly shows that the contemporary perspective also enters into the interpretation of Scripture, and this applies equally to the study of patristic and scholastic theology, to name only two.

Sanctifying grace and the theological virtues. The modern anthropological view that the human person is essentially fitted for encounter with his fellow men and can possess himself fully only in and through the act of giving himself to the other person has also resulted in grace coming to be seen more in the light of an "intersubjective" relationship. Not only do we experience sanctifying grace even more clearly and explicitly than before as a personal living communion with God, but we also tend to give increased scope to the personal character of grace in our systematic thinking about this reality. Our attention is more closely focussed nowadays on the truly reciprocal relationship of action and reaction between the divine and the human partner involved, while still maintaining the distinctively transcendent manner of God's reaction to man. This has meant that the structure of the treatise on grace is no longer based on the case of the conferment of grace upon immature children, but on the "encounter" between fully grown man and the living God in Christ. The re-

ciprocal relationship existing between God and ourselves
has thus been given a central position in the doctrine of
grace. The central truth of sanctifying grace is now seen
to be the idea that God allows himself to be personally
loved by man. The very essence of grace is to be found in
this *unio amoris,* and "created grace" is only the ontological
(but necessary) implication of this.

This return not only to the biblical and patristic conception of grace—and, at least in its essence, also to the scholastic view—but also, and above all, to the concept of grace
that is ordinarily held by all Christians by virtue of their
living experience, has resulted in our once again becoming
aware of the (perhaps implicit or, more accurately expressed,
implied) supernatural element of experience both of faith
and of hope and love. This is indeed an authentic experience, the very heart of the life of grace, but it is at the same
time an element that cannot normally be pointed out here
and now in our human experience. It is nonetheless present
in a special manner that is constantly appearing in a different light in the act of faith, the act of hope and the act of
love. If this element were not present somehow in man's
actual experience (*in actu exercito*), it would not be possible for us to see how these theological virtues are really
based on a *supernatural* motive and not, for example, on a
natural idea of God's infallibility, of his universal power and
love, as we, as creatures, are able to some extent to grasp it.
Here too, it would be wrong to make any cleavage between
"ontology" and "psychology" and impossible to place grace
as an ontic category completely outside the sphere of the
human psyche, although this experience is only brought
about in our natural humanity and is thus not a "miniature
beatific vision." Moreover, both the Bible and patristic
theology—and even scholastic theology which, in the context
of the act of faith, referred to a *iudicium per modum con-*

naturalitatis in grace—pointed repeatedly to this aspect of experience in the three theological virtues. Nonetheless, in order to come to full and truly reflective *Catholic* understanding of this aspect of experience in the life of grace, we should have to wait until the time was ripe for mankind, growing in truth, to be able to see conceptual knowledge not simply as identical with human knowledge but as only one, albeit indispensable, element of the sum of human knowledge.

In this way, we have come to a greater awareness of the view that there is a personal, inward divine invitation at the source of our consent in faith, a grace that inwardly draws us to faith, a grace through which we experience in ourselves—although in an obscure manner—an inclination to believe what is presented to us by the Church as the Word of God—the *initium fidei*. Thus we hear God's "inward conversation," his revelation of himself. It is only by virtue of this divine conversation in grace that we are able to trust in his word and extend the grace of faith to, and elaborate it into a free personal consent in faith with, the revelation that the Church presents to us.

This personal character and this "implied" aspect of experience are also present in the virtue of hope. Within the already established attitude of faith, Christian hope also has its origin only in a personal address, acting as a guarantee, by God who inwardly invites us to hope—that is, to trust in him. This invitation brings about in us an obscure experience of God's promise and pledge of his saving power which invites us to place our life in his hands. It is this element of grace—the "beginning of hope"—that brings about in us, probably in spite of conflicting human feelings, an inception of childlike trust that is difficult to define and which we then, in the act of divine hope, extend to and elaborate into a free, personal decision and commitment.

It is only in this grace of hope, and thus in this reciprocal relationship between God and ourselves, that our hoping, as an act of grace, can be grounded. (This is so even though we can also, as in the case of faith, provide from without, as it were, a certain discreet and reasonable justification of this hope as a human act.)

Finally, Christian love as a theological virtue also goes back to an initiative in grace on the part of God, who "first loved us" (1 John iv. 19) and who invites us to communion in love. It is in and through this inward divine invitation (which we can never, as in the case of faith and hope, divorce from our total human experience of life and our encounter with everything that addresses us in this world) that we experience a movement of the heart that can never be precisely situated in our human psyche, a movement through which we begin to "feel" ourselves as sons of a Father. This is the "beginning of love," and this "affective knowledge" of God's inviting love which is brought about by grace is something to which we give our consent in a free act of love, by means of which we here and now enter into personal, living communion with God.

Let me reiterate, then, that this divine invitation to faith, hope and love is, as it were, closely interwoven with our total experience as human beings. That is why it is not possible, in ordinary cases, to point to it here and now. However, the element of experience, which in the "ordinary" Christian life is only present in a veiled manner in the background of the human consciousness as a magnet attracting everything to itself, comes to the forefront of the consciousness in the case of the mystic life. But in both cases the structure is the same: it is personal, and this means, as far as our personal relationship with God is concerned, *theologal*. It is because this theologal life is not purely conceptual that the "covenant" character—the essential I-thou relationship which typifies the theological virtues—although certainly not denied in the past (all the greatest scholastics of the high Middle Ages were quite explicit in their affirmation of it) was undoubtedly "forgotten" in the later scholastic systematisation of Christian life, though not in the practice of Christian life at this period. This is why there was, at this time, a too one-sided concentration of attention on "created grace." It is true that unless created grace is accepted, the reciprocal theologal relationship between God and man becomes meaningless, but it is not created grace with which we are really concerned in our Christian life.

In our own time justice is once more gradually being done in theological synthesis to the christological and pneumatic character of grace and of the theological virtues, precisely because we have come explicitly to recognise the personal nature of grace. This has also led to the settlement at long last of a very old question, never fully resolved in scholastic theology. Because the scholastic theologians made too sharp a distinction between the treatise on God (*De Deo uno*) and the treatise on the Trinity (*De Deo trino*), it was difficult for them to reconcile the life of grace, seen as a "sharing in God's nature," with the personal relationship of man, informed by grace, with the three divine persons in their oneness and their distinctness. When, however, it is more clearly established that the one living God is the three persons, and grace, on the other hand, is seen as a personal encounter with God (an encounter that nonetheless still takes place within faith), then it is at once clear that the presence of God and man to each other—that is, grace—is, of its very nature, a personal encounter with the three persons in their distinctness and their divine oneness. Any other sharing in the "divine nature" is thus excluded by the fact itself. *Personal* communion with the divine nature is impossible without a personal communion with the three divine persons. What is more, a personal communion is never an encounter with a "nature"; it is an encounter with a definite person! Thus, the old question as to whether we have "only" a *consortium divinae naturae* through grace, or have "in addition" a personal relationship with each of the three divine persons is really a false question, since the one is the other.

The Church and her sacraments. The modern idea of anthropological incarnation has certainly been of great assistance in throwing light on the mystery of the Church. It cannot be denied that the ecclesiology of the last century was remarkably dualistic—on the one hand, there were theologians who regarded the Church as a mystery without reference to her social structure and her historical existence and, on the other, historians who described events in the Church's life purely in terms of their temporal aspect. In contrast to this sharp division, the Church is nowadays increasingly considered as a mystery appearing on this earth in a historical form, so that in this sphere too the older dualism is being overcome. Both in her institutional form and in the life of the baptised Christian in this world the Church is now seen and experienced as the visible form on earth of Christ's redemptive grace.

This has resulted in greater justice being done to the institutional aspect of the Church and in a greater opportunity being offered for a clearer understanding of the ambiguity of this institutional aspect. The communion of grace with Christ and the communion of those who believe with each other is "embodied" in the Church in institutional structures and at the same time fully realised in this incarnation. In the natural social life of man, the human person can, because of his essential incarnation, experience his communion with other men only in expressive acts of love through which he encounters others directly via physical nature. Built up on the *unio amoris*, the human community of persons is therefore concretely realised in all kinds of structures of economic, social and cultural institutions for social and human welfare. Spiritual or personal communion among men is fully possible only by incarnation in structures of this kind. Although the Church as a community has an essentially different source, this anthropological structure nonetheless continues to have its effects in the Church as an institution. The interpersonal relationships, our communion of grace with Christ and with other believers, are made incarnate, and fully realised by this incarnation, in the institutional structures of the Church. In this way, the Church is, even in her institutional aspects, truly the visible form of the active presence in grace of Christ among us.

On the other hand, however, the institution is, even in the human community, essentially characterised by a certain ambiguity. It would be quite wrong to see the institutional structures of the human community on earth only as an expression and an embodiment of the spiritual communion. It is an essential feature of the incarnation that the human spirit embodies itself in data which are in themselves not human, but which acquire, through this incarnation, a share in humanity. This means that the institutional aspects of the human community also display a certain *independence* in respect of interpersonal relationships, and are not a pure expression of spiritual communion. The science that we call empirical sociology is both possible and useful because of this.

This applies equally within the separate form that is the Church. This very independence of the institutional aspects makes it possible, for example, for someone to be really a member of the community of the Church and to receive the sacraments—to "practice," as it is called—while he is in fact outside the communion of love. The whole theology of the validity of sacraments which can be unfruitful, of the saving power of the priest's actions within the Church which is independent of the sanctity of the priest, and so on —all this theology is based, from the anthropological point of view at least, on this distinctively earthly quality of institutional structures. That is why a religious sociology of Church life is possible. It also indicates that, to whatever degree the *institutional* incarnation of the Church may form an essential feature of the Church here *on earth*, these earthly, institutional aspects will nonetheless pass away. On the other hand, the heavenly Church will not be purely spiritual. The visible incarnation of the Church will outlive time; only in heaven will it be, in and through pneumatic nature, the pure expression of our communion of love and grace with God in Christ. All this has resulted in the modern theologian's gaining a clearer insight into the relationship between religion, Christianity and the function of the Church. It has also meant that we have achieved a more subtle understanding of the practice of Christianity within the Church, without losing sight of the fact that it is only in the Church that the full, living form of religion desired by God is present, and that all religion is inwardly attuned to the life of the Church.

It is probably quite well known that new vistas have been disclosed to theological reflection on the sacraments and the liturgy of the Church by this renewed anthropological understanding, which has, moreover, some relation to the biblical view of "body and soul." Of course, Catholics have always believed in the sacramental reality signified by the central rites of the celebration of the Eucharist and of the other sacraments. But we see now, even more explicitly than Christians saw in the centuries immediately preceding the present one, that the sacraments are not "things" but the characteristically human form of man's encounter with the

living Christ. In addition, we want once again to experience
sacramental worship as a direct expression of this encounter
with the Lord and once again actively to experience the
public worship of the Church—the liturgy as such, that is—
as the cult of the entire community. For this reason more
attention has been devoted to the power of expression of the
sacramental sign, and the modern anthropological insight
into the essential incarnation of man has resulted in a more
finely shaded view of the doctrine of the *signum*, thanks
to the phenomenological analysis of human activity. This
has also led to a deeper existential understanding of Aquinas's central principle, *sacramentum est in genere signi,*
the sacrament is in the nature of a sign, even so far as the
Eucharist is concerned. Here too, we have become more
clearly aware of the fact that the sacrifice of the Mass, as
a communal sacrifice and meal, is, thanks to transubstantiation, a *sacramentum-signum*. This means that the communal
character of the Mass must *appear* from the sign itself. And
although it may be true that a "private" Mass, with or
without a server, is still really a communal sacrifice from
the theological point of view, it is equally true that the
sacramental character of my faith demands that I should
see this in what is taking place before me. And this visible
quality cannot be actively experienced in a "private" Mass.
In the form of the "private Mass," the *sacramental* significance of the Eucharist was based on a very narrow foundation—a foundation that was just wide enough for it to remain
within the limits of Catholic orthodoxy. In the same spirit
of reappraisal of the power of expression of the sacramental
sign, our "approaching the Lord's table"—that is, our coming to the sacrificial altar—is also seen as the expression
of being *together* one in the Lord of the Church, so that
the act of communion is now separated as little as possible
from the communal celebration of the sacrifice.

The liturgical movement has, however, not yet assimilated these dogmatic insights. Some Catholics even pin their faith to a number of practical changes. I agree with Dr. C. Bouman's observation that there has, up to now, been no more than a sincere concern in the direction of liturgical revival. But nothing of importance has ever come about in the Church without a background of such a concern, and we are now waiting for an attempt to give a liturgically expressive form to our present-day religious awareness.

The eschatological expectation of the future. The influence of the new anthropological insights can be felt most strongly perhaps in the sphere of eschatology, a theological treatise which is at present, to quote Hans Urs von Balthasar's scornful comment, "closed for complete reconstruction." Of course the image is exaggerated, but it has a point to make if we apply it not so much to the scientific eschatology of the past as to the notions about eschatology that believers in general have derived from the scientific study of the subject. Our theological ideas about heaven, hell and purgatory, the soul "separated" from the body, the interim in the post-terrestrial state before the resurrection, the last judgment and the *parousia* are all, at least in their representational aspects, being fundamentally "demythologised" in the light of our more sharply defined insights into the essential correlation between the spirit which communicates itself to the body and the body which shares in this spirit. These realities are now rightly seen as first of all interior to man, while they preserve, at least from the resurrection onwards, their truly *physical* significance. They are seen as the *human* implications of our final communion of grace with God in Christ or of our final falling away from this communion. The resurrection of the body especially is no longer seen as an incomprehensible gift added to the beatific vision; it is seen as an essential incarnation of this vision, which then begins to exist in a genuinely human condition involving emotion and awareness, as the beginning of heavenly intersubjectivity between all those who are co-recipients of grace in a glorified world; in a word, as the interhuman incarnation of the communion of grace with the God of heaven and earth and the God, above all, of all created persons.

The method employed in studying the last things has in particular been more sharply defined. In the light of the anthropological view that human life is of its very nature a life which, on the basis of the past, is moving in the present towards a future, and that the present is therefore the future which is realising itself now, we have come with greater justification to accept the idea, on the one hand, that the historical, non-mythical character of the end of the world cannot be denied, but, on the other, that the *eschata* will be nothing but the implications of man's communion of grace with God in the mode of completion. All eschatological statements, therefore, have their source in our present existence in grace, seen in its essential orientation towards its ultimate fulfilment. In this way, gradually the theological affirmation is finding acceptance that an eschatological treatise can tell us no more than we already know, theologically, in christology, in the treatise on grace and in the *theological* treatise on man in the context of creation. The modern treatise on the *eschata* is in this way able to remain free from false predictions of the future and from the apocalyptic oracles with which popular preachers sometimes try to catch their listeners' attention.

Bad Influences

The new anthropological views have unfortunately also had a bad effect on some theological questions. This has come about because full weight has not been given to man's spiritual being in the versions of these philosophical views which are the most widespread. Such emphasis has been laid on the essential incarnation that the real transcendence of the human spirit (albeit in an incarnation on this earth) has, in general, not been fully taken into account. The view of M. Merleau-Ponty, for example, in which a trans-ascendency of the human spirit, as J. Wahl calls it, has no place has had a strong unconscious influence on many modern theologians, with the result that various minor crypto-heresies are at present going round among Catholic theologians and laymen. Many theologians no longer accept the *anima separata* (although they dare not say so aloud), and for this reason these scholars also deny the "interim" and, partly perhaps under the influence of Bultmann's problem, make the first moment after death coincide with the resurrection. This has at the same time resulted in the general judgment, the *parousia*, the resurrection and the social dimensions of salvation being stripped of their true biblical significance.

Another unfortunate result of the new insights has been such a great attachment to the existential categories of intersubjectivity and encounter that the *ontological* implications of the communion of grace with God have been completely neglected. This has meant a ready denial, with a wink in the direction of reformed Christians, of what is termed *gratia creata*, the usefulness and meaning of which is no longer seen. This clearly reveals the lack of metaphysics in modern phenomenology. But these examples of how theology has gone off the rails can also be explained by an excessive reaction against misrepresentations occurring in our theological manuals, in which the *anima separata* is often presented as an angel and *gratia creata* is dealt with at great length in physical categories and the personal aspect of grace obscured.

Other theologians have similarly gone off the rails in connection with the *kenōsis*, or Christ's emptying of himself. Some have given such exaggerated emphasis to Christ's "human condition" that the insight according to which this Man is really "full of grace" and even is God in a human manner is simply disregarded. The deep, inscrutable character of the man Jesus *as a mystery* is forgotten—the content of truth in the Alexandrian christology is sacrificed in this Antiochian tendency. The transcendence of the incarnation of Christ is thereby insufficiently perceived. The incarnation is identified with being completely man—*la présence du Christ au monde*, the presence of Christ in the world, in which it is often overlooked that this presence is a *redeeming* presence. Many having responsibilities in the practical spheres of pastoral care and the apostolate have slipped off the rails as a consequence. It would, however, be wrong to regard the whole renewal of present-day theology with suspicion simply because of a few errors of this kind.

THE HISTORICAL CHARACTER
OF HUMAN LIFE

Good Influences

A third characteristic which, although dating from an earlier period (Hegel, the German romantic movement, Bergson), is closely connected with this phenomenology is the discovery of the historical dimension of human consciousness and the essential historical character of human life. It may well be significant in this context that the term "salvation history" was almost unknown in Catholic theology before the Second World War. The reference "salvation history" does not, to the best of my knowledge, appear in a single theological dictionary, with the exception of the recently issued part of the second edition of the *Lexikon für Theologie und Kirche*. In philosophical lexicons and dictionaries, on the other hand, quite substantial entries appeared at a far earlier date under the heading *Histoire* or *Geschichte*. In any case, the relatively recent insight into the historical aspect of revelation has radically changed the entire plan of every theological treatise.

God accomplishes in history his intentions with regard to man. God's activity is history in that it reveals itself, and it reveals itself by becoming history. Revelation is a growing historical process set in motion anonymously in the concrete life of every human being in the world. It acquired a more concrete form in Israel and finally reached the constitutive phase of its maturity in Christ and in the early apostolic Church. Whenever a present-day theologian wishes to enquire about the content of divine revelation in connection, for example, with faith in creation, he turns first of all to Israel, to see how this people—and they precisely as the people of God—experienced the reality of creation and interpreted it in the religious sense. Then he considers Christ and how he, conscious of his Sonship, actively experienced this reality. Finally, he investigates the way in which the earliest Christians, as the people of God redeemed in Christ, concretely experienced and interpreted this same reality of creation.

The theologian does not, therefore, examine directly the so-called *nuda vox Dei*, as Karl Barth proposes. It is, in any case, impossible to see how he can do this. Faith is an essential correlative to revelation, and God accomplishes his revelation *in a dialogue* with mankind. The theologian therefore considers in the first place the report or the account of the way in which God, in his intervention within

salvation history, allowed a religious meaning to be given
to creation or the *eschata,* for example, and allowed these to
be experienced in a religious way by his chosen people. This
at once distinguishes the modern treatise on, for example,
the creation from the *De Deo Creante* of our theological
manuals, which is often no more than a disguised theodicy.
In the modern treatise light is thrown, as it were from the
perspective of the history of salvation, on the mystery of the
philosophical idea of creation, which is assumed as a natural
praeambulum fidei, a predisposition for faith. Something of
the distinctively divine manner of this unique activity that
we call creation, *creare ex nihilo,* is thereby illuminated.

In this we are, however, conscious of the fact that the
whole of the history of salvation is looking forward towards
Christ. The theological source, the *locus theologicus,* even
of faith in the creation is really the personal, human history
of the historical Christ. This applies to every theological
treatise, and the consequence has been a complete renewal
of the theological method—in contrast to the method employed by previous generations of theologians, we now come
to a *theologia* via an *oikonomia.* The *oikonomia* of salvation
is the means by which we come to a *theologia.* Christian immortality, for example, is thus seen to be quite different
from immortality in the philosophical sense, although the
latter forms the necessary preamble to the former. Philosophical immortality is an *implication of the human state of
being a person,* whereas Christian immortality is an *implication of our communion of grace* with the living God in
Christ. This Christian insight has grown in and from the
history of Israel's salvation in dialogue with God and in
and from living Christian experience, an experience which
enabled Paul to say that nothing could separate us from
Christ, not even death (Rom. viii. 38–39). Christian im-

mortality therefore essentially implies, via Christ, a relationship with glorified physical nature, and is quite different from the pure "continued existence of the soul," which is assumed in this, because otherwise the personal identity between the man on earth and the man in heaven is endangered. Speculative theology therefore automatically acquires a new form in the light of salvation history, whereas, in the past, theological treatises were often given a philosophical emphasis, and philosophy, on the other hand, was frequently given a theological slant.

This awareness of the historical dimension in human life and our resulting interest in the history of salvation has not only changed the plan of every theological treatise. It has also opened up many new perspectives in the content of faith, and has even led to the emergence of all kinds of new treatises. Not only in eschatology, for example, actively forming the basis for a *theology* of Church history—a similar development is also taking place in the creation of a theology of earthly values, of history, of work, of the physical cosmos as the environment of man, and so on.

It also goes without saying that our new insight into the historical character of the *actus humanus* is of enormous importance in the sphere of moral theology—that is, in our understanding of the natural law, of mortal and venial sin and of asceticism and mysticism. In this context too, we have gained an important insight into the existence of a certain, although inadequate, distinction between man's basic personal will and his separate actions. Furthermore, we have come more consistently to appreciate that there is a parallel in the order of good to what is known, in the order of evil, as mortal sin and venial sin—namely, an *actus humanus graviter bonus* and an *actus humanus leviter bonus*. This insight is of enormous importance in connection with the

reception of the sacraments, as well as, for example, in connection with judging the validity of a marriage (as an *actus
graviter humanus*).

Bad Influences

Here too (and how could it be otherwise, in view of the
fact that all progress in theology presents us with fresh op-
portunities for error?), the new theology does not always
keep strictly to the rails. And once again, it is a faulty
philosophical view that has produced a one-sided theology.
Phenomenology, which correctly stresses the historical character of all human life, has not always appreciated the fact
that this historical character in man is accompanied by a
consciousness of time in the strict sense of the word. And a
consciousness of time implies a rising above time. This does
not mean that we somehow come to stand outside time and
the world, but that there is a *transhistorical orientation* in
the historical character of our human life. The result of
this misunderstanding has been that speculative theology is
frequently neglected. Recent theology is often no more than
salvation history—it is identified with christology.

A typical example of this tendency to go no further than
the *oikonomia* of salvation and not to see a *theologia* in the
light of this *oikonomia* is the recent work *Fragen der Theologie heute*. One treatise is missing from this theological
work, which is otherwise well conceived in its marked
tendency towards salvation history. This is the *De Deo uno
et trino*, the treatise on God. To me this seems to be symp-
tomatic of our lack of insight into the fact that we in some
way or another really transcend the historical character of
human life. But here too, reaction is at the back of the
exaggeration. The theological manuals were often too rigid
in their presentation of a *theologia* without *oikonomia*, and

it is inevitable that a number of scholars will react against this by denying any place to *theologia* in their renewed interest in the economy of salvation and, in so doing, step outside the limits of the Catholic faith.

RECOGNITION OF THE DISTINCTIVE CHARACTER OF THE RELIGIOUS ELEMENT AND THE CASE FOR A CERTAIN SECULARISATION

A fourth characteristic, which is also related to the phenomenological view of the essential incarnation of the human person, is our present-day awareness of man's task within this world and the tendency towards secularisation. Natural legal structures have been rediscovered. We are all familiar with mocking observations of the following sort. Whereas in the Middle Ages processions led by the clergy went through the cities in times of plague, today we prescribe isolation and the necessary drugs in such emergencies, and the epidemic is quickly stopped—but in the Middle Ages it would get worse after a penitential procession. Whereas men used to pray "From storm, thunder and lightning deliver us, Lord," modern man has a lightning conductor installed on his house, and that seems to work better too. The vital question concerning the fitness of this world for habitation and the meaning and the future of life is at this moment central. Modern man takes his life into his own hands—he is *faber suiipsius*. His power even extends as far as the world of the stars and planets, which in the past was deified. All this has resulted in spontaneous faith—the "faith of the Breton peasant woman"—being profoundly disturbed. Faith itself seems have been seriously impaired by it.

I feel, however, that this modern situation, which is increasingly forcing believers to live in a state of "diaspora," has above all a *purifying* function. We had allowed faith

to become devalued, so that it had become little more than
a life-raft in emergencies. We had become insensitive to the
complete transcendence of revelation over our significance
within this world. Our intimacy with the supernatural,
which is more real to us than the chair we sit on, was not
always the intimacy of someone who knows himself to be
secure. We have tended to see God too much as a function
of our life, rather than seeing our life as something in his
service. We had become insufficiently aware of the fact that
prayer for temporal things is incomprehensible if we limit
ourselves to the purely natural standpoint of the relationship between "cause and effect." That is why the claim is
nowadays always being made that prayer for temporal things
is meaningless. The Church, however, takes a different view,
because she experiences the reality of God not only naturally
but also supernaturally, religiously. If the God with whom
we associate personally is the God of creation who is
interested in everything that happens in the world, and if,
on the other hand, this world, in which we are so fully
involved, also interests us, then it goes without saying that we
are bound to speak spontaneously, in our personal encounters with the living God in prayer, about those very things,
which are of as great interest to him as they are to us. It is
only in the light of the reciprocal relationship existing
between God and ourselves thanks to grace that there can
really be any question of a distinctively divine personal reaction to man's personal asking. Even in temporal things,
God wants to be man's father in Christ and Christ wants
to place his mastery over things in the service of the man
who believes in it (without, however, wishing to replace
man and his culture). In the past we have not always seen
this in its true perspective. We have, moreover, often been
shortsighted in this regard. We have been anxious about

the most minor temporal concerns, but more important things—international tensions, the future of our secular world, the new society that is being fashioned (to a very great extent outside the sphere of Christianity), distress in the underdeveloped countries, and so on—are also "temporal things" and just as important as fine weather or rain for the crops. We were not wrong to pray for the latter, but we were wrong to make no mention in our prayers of the former, those other "temporal" things which, even from the secular point of view, may be more important than our daily bread—as though God had nothing to do with them!

We have now come to acknowledge that the Christian's work in the world does not exclusively have heaven in view, he is responsible also for this earth and its future. The Christian is aware now that, although he is called to a supernatural destiny, he must nonetheless remain faithful to the world he is living in—he is fully responsible for its future. He accepts, along with the world, all the laws and all the possibilities that are implied in his existence in it. His attitude towards human society and its whole culture is one of positive affirmation. He is conscious of his intimate association in this world with all men, and there is nothing to prevent him from co-operating with anyone if this co-operation is directed towards the preservation and the development of human values and does not involve him in evil. In all this activity, he is *in faith*—his secular concern for this world is a Christian task. It is, therefore, the aim of Christianity to give a form to this world. Now as never before in the past we are aware that man is not simply a piece of nature, but really and radically a subject, making his own history—*faber suiipsius*—on a situational basis, although this basis no longer appears to be as firmly fixed as we once thought. This inevitably has repercussions on the

social, economic and political action of Catholics. Basing
our argument on authority as the regulating principle, we
Catholics have, for example, too often tended to reason that
the authority of the State should be exclusively concerned
with the preservation of the existing order and not be the
creative subject of real structural reforms. We have frequently covered unjust systems of law with the cloak of
so-called charity and have been all too readily inclined to
look on the outbreak of world or state revolution as the
coming of the beast of the Apocalypse. The consideration
which we have neglected, in such cases, is that usually revolution is in some sense an expression of a genuine longing
for a more humane world, and our too frequent reaction
has been to resist the emergence of this new world by appealing to the so-called God of the order of creation. *Homo
faber suiipsius*—man himself, as a subject, has the task of
making the world a dwelling-place fit for and worthy of
man, a place in which the human community of persons
can grow, in justice and love and through grace, into a
communion of saints.

The theology of the laity—the theology of the significance
and the real place of the laity in the Church—is also closely
related to all this. Of course, we should not restrict the
role of the layman to his task in the world. In the theological
sense of the word, "layman" means the baptised member of
the community of faith of the Church. Through baptism,
the layman (regarded as a category within the Church) has,
like the priest, an ecclesial and sacral task. The only difference between the two is that the clergy fulfils this sacral
task in the mode of the apostolic authority, whereas the
laity fulfil it as the "people of God." For this reason every
layman is jointly responsible with the clergy for the life of
the Church. Lay people have their own word to say and

their own actions to perform in the Church. By their in-
corporation into the Church, "the sign set up among the
nations," they share in its essential function—that is, to
give a visible form to grace in their whole lives, and thus
to be themselves an effective and visible sign of grace in the
world. The theological definition of the laity is thus to be
found in their membership here and now of the Church,
with an ecclesial mission. It is, of course, true that this ecclesial mission, which the layman receives by virtue of his
baptism, is given to a *man*—that is, to someone who, as a
man, has a meaningful task to fulfil in this world; it is consequently given to a man who has the task of working for
a humane world order. But the layman does not possess *this*
mission by virtue of his baptism. What his baptism gives
him is the task of *integrating* this worldly role into his communion of grace with God in Christ. For the layman, then,
this worldly task forms a part of his total religious attitude
to life. He has to integrate his secular life into his faith,
which means that an "apostolic secular" existence is the
province of the Christian layman.

It is, of course, understandable that all kinds of deviations
occur in this sphere too, although these often constitute a
danger for authentic faith. The worldly aspect of the religious attitude sometimes results in a misunderstanding of
the transcendent aspects of Christianity. The "evangelical
counsels," especially virginity, and the value of prayer in
itself have been disputed by some scholars who feel uncom-
fortable in the presence of these aspects of Christianity. The
authority of the hierarchy of the Church is appreciated only
in its motivation, the autonomy of the structures relating
to this world is not always seen in the perspective of the
religious life-destiny, and so on. These deviations, which
occur in good faith, are inherent in any growing pains, but

they must be overcome if the element of truth in the contemporary process of secularisation is to be integrated into *Catholic* truth.

THE ECUMENICAL CHARACTER OF PRESENT-DAY DOGMATIC THEOLOGY

Now more than ever in the past there is conscious dialogue between men of differing views and beliefs. As a result there has also been a new growth in tolerance. Theology has moved in the same direction. To a far greater extent than hitherto, Catholic theologians are engaging actively in conversation with their counterparts not only in the other Christian churches, but also in the other great world religions and even—although this seems to be coming about much more slowly—with modern atheistic humanists. This is, of course, also connected with our recognition of the part which *perspective* plays in human consciousness, a recognition which, although it involves the danger of our becoming rather indifferent to objective truth, nevertheless makes us fundamentally alert to the content of truth in what others think and believe. Furthermore, the full content of truth in any partial truth can be affirmed only when this partial truth is integrated into the total truth. Every partial affirmation of truth acts as a spur to the discovery within its own context of the wholeness natural to truth. The arguments of those whose thought and faith is different from ours look, to a certain degree, objectively in the direction of catholicity—they contain an objective dynamism which is often revealed in subjective experience as an openness to, a seeking and a desire for, conversation.

Modern dogmatic theologians are fully aware of this, with the result that their work is now characterized by a markedly ecumenical orientation whereas, before, the construction of all its parts clearly formed an anti-heretical synthesis. Dogmatic theology has thereby achieved a greater inner balance, in which "forgotten truths"—that is, aspects of faith which had been thrust into the background by the reaction against the abandonment of other dogmatic elements—have once more been accorded their rightful place.

Dogmatic theology has, however, become more ecumenical not only by abandoning the anti-heretical tendency of the earlier dogmatic synthesis, but also by considering the ecclesial problem of divided Christianity and by engaging in positive dialogue with other churches. Confrontation with, for example, a living, strongly religious reformed practice has forced Catholic theologians once more to reflect positively about the ecumenical character of the Catholic faith in all its aspects. As a Christian category, the *oikoumenē* is a gift of God to the *Catholica,* a gift that is to be found in the fact that the one Church of Christ is, by divine predestination, the home of all men. This gift cannot be lost, even by divisions and schisms. But it can be obscured, on the one hand by divisions and on the other by internal infidelity.

In addition, new problems have been raised by the fact that the divided churches have for centuries pursued their own historical course, so that each of them has developed further along *independent* lines. Apart from the essential structures which the Lord gave to his Church *ne varietur* (although in growth and movement as far as their concrete form is concerned), the visible figures of these forms have not stayed the same throughout the course of time. The Church is constantly making herself incarnate in elements belonging to this earth, and these elements are to some extent transitory. Moreover, every period in the history of the Catholic Church has its own special emphases—in each period, one thing is given greater prominence, another less, just as each period has its own emphases in piety (the

so-called *metabletica* of the religious life). This applies
equally to the other Christian churches. Thus, the dogmatic
differences between the various Christian churches can be
increased and made more complicated by all kinds of forms
and concrete emphases which are not, as such, essential to
the authentic religious life of the Church.

In the case of the Catholic Church, for example, we are
aware of the emergence, alongside the deeper, inviolable
significance of the *Romana Ecclesia,* of the so-called "Ro-
mish" characteristics in Catholic piety, especially since the
Counter-Reformation, characteristics which are, in my opinion, to a great extent conditioned purely by historical circumstances. In this sense, we may correctly speak of a *"coming* ecumenical Church," meaning that the coming *form* of
the Catholic Church will have to manifest its *oikoumenē*
in a special way. It is precisely for this reason that a growing
concern is being felt in the Church and in Catholic theology
for the need to strip the structure and form of the modern
Church of everything that obscures her *oikoumenē,* so that
the one Bride of Christ may once again be clearly recognised
by all. Catholics do, of course, sometimes go to extremes
and some, as Pope John expressed it, will be satisfied in
their desire for a complete change in the Church's concrete
form only when the pope casts nets again in the sea of
Gennesaret! But even those who do not deny the sober law
of historical growth are conscious of a clear need to give
a new form to the Church.

Certainly the Catholic Church can never renounce her
belief that the deposit of faith was entrusted to her care. On
the other hand, however, we cannot pretend that Protestant,
Anglican and Orthodox Christians have simply to come to
us in order to gain everything from us and that we have
nothing to learn from them. In giving a concrete form to
our deposit of faith, there can certainly be an *integration* of

the other Christian churches. It is in fact a question of rectifying those aspects of Catholic thought and action that have become too one-sided, and of reinstating certain aspects of faith that have, in the course of history, been forced, because of our traditionally anti-heretical attitude, from their central place onto the periphery, or vice-versa, at least in their visible form and in the concrete manner in which they have been experienced in the life of the Church.

If a Catholic is converted to reformed Christianity, we call this infidelity, because he has objectively abandoned a part of the Christian inheritance. On the other hand, the conversion of a reformed Christian to Catholicism is not regarded, from the Catholic point of view, as infidelity to the Christian deposit of faith of the reformed churches. (Even from the reformed point of view, this conversion can only be called infidelity with regard to what is "exclusively" Protestant.) This Christian deposit in itself is originally Catholic. It will be found again in the Catholic Church, integrated into what was in a certain sense renounced by the Reformation. On the other hand, however, we are then faced with the problem of how the concrete forms given to the positive treasury of Christian faith by the Protestant churches (forms which in themselves may be called just as good as Catholic forms) can be accorded their proper place within the present form of the Catholic Church. Certain authentically Christian forms which may, after all, be only weakly represented in the Catholic Church are given a prominent place in the religious experience of the Protestant communions. (Examples of these are bible reading and the holy desire to hear the Word proclaimed.) It is impossible to cancel out the past in the history of Christianity —this cannot be done for psychological reasons, but above all it cannot be done for religious and dogmatic reasons. This in turn raises the question as to whether Protestant

Christians, in view of the form which developed within their own historical traditions and which they have given to the originally Catholic deposit of faith (a form which cannot, in itself, be explained by what is "exclusive" to reformed Christianity), will here and now find room to live in the *Catholica* so that they can really feel at home with their own positively Christian past.

Reformed Christians—especially theologians—who are in living contact with the new developments in Catholic theology are often astonished by the fact that very little trace of these new emphases can be discovered in the concrete life of Catholics within the Church. This causes them to react in one of two ways—either they think that these Catholic theologians, though unquestionably theologians, are not really Catholic theologians, but rather offshoots of the Catholic Church; or they wonder whether there is really not such a thing as "Roman equivocation," in which two separate standards exist—a theology for domestic use—authentic in its private sphere—and a theology for export and expansion. I have put it in an extreme form, but I have experienced reactions of this kind. The after-care of those who are converted from Protestantism to Catholicism is therefore one of the great pastoral problems, and this applies perhaps more to the Netherlands than, for example, to Germany. Such conversions often result in disillusionment or spiritual tensions, at least in the case of those average converts who are not trained in theology. That is why we can only hope, in the spirit of Pope John XXIII, that—without doing violence to the never very rapid process of development of our historical humanity—the years after the Vatican Council will honour the authentic gains of the new Catholic theology and give them evangelical expression in the renewal of the outward form of the Church.

APPENDIX:
THE NON-CONCEPTUAL
INTELLECTUAL DIMENSION IN
OUR KNOWLEDGE OF GOD
ACCORDING TO AQUINAS

THE PROBLEM

The objective value of our knowledge of God is, according to a Thomist view subsequent to Scotus, based on the abstract character of what are called "transcendental concepts." In the words of Pénido, whose work is typical of this tradition and has become it classic expression:

The concept is absolute and attributable to God because it is abstract. At the same time, however, it enables us to know about God simply what he has proportionately in common with his creatures.[1]

This tendency calls the *transcendentalia,* like every concept, a *universale,* but they are characterized by the fact that their unity does not constitute a *univocum,* but a *universale proportionale.* In other words, it constitutes a *ratio abstracta* which nonetheless includes, in an actual (although implicit) way, the creaturely and the divine modes of realisation, so that the concept itself is called analogical in the manner of a *proportionalitas.* The unity of the analogical concept is called a *unum secundum quid* and a *diversum*

[1] M. Pénido, *Le rôle de l'analogie en théologie dogmatique,* Paris 1931, 123.

simpliciter, or, in accordance with Suarez' interpretation, *simpliciter unum, secundum quid diversum.* As a result, when we think or speak about God, we no longer really use creaturely concepts, but *grasp* God himself notionally in and through the proportionally one, transcendental, but nonetheless abstract, concepts.[2]

Pénido's contention gave rise to a good deal of controversy, led by Descoqs, Sertillanges, Blanche, Balthasar, Valensin, and de Raeymaeker. The problem was narrowed down to the question as to whether the *analogia proportionalitatis propriae* too included a prime analogate. All the arguments against Pénido took the same basic assumption as their starting-point, namely, that the analogical unity was a conceptual unity, and from that point questioned the implication of an *analogia attributionis intrinsecae* in the so-called "proper analogy" of Cajetan.

The first epistemologically critical study of these findings was made by Maréchal.[3] He started from the Kantian view that a speculative, intuitive grasp of reality is impossible if the human intellect is not essentially intuitive—in whatever way, provided only that this intuition is an *intellectual* intuition. This led him to the necessity of a critical justification of the traditional doctrine of analogy.

For, if the claim is made that the transcendental relationship of analogy is known, and if a legitimate raising of the "significa-

---

[2] One typical and classic passage should suffice: "No theological research can achieve successful results—escaping from metaphorism and anthropomorphism—unless we accept straight away, in our mind, a capacity for abstraction which allows us to think in transcendental terms. The transcendental idea of goodness is no longer formally (but only proportionately) the concept of created goodness, and it is this idea which we apply proportionally to God. It is in and through this universal idea that we know subsistent goodness" (Pénido, 189).

[3] J. Maréchal, *Le point de départ de la métaphysique,* Louvain and Paris 1920ff. (five volumes).

tion" of certain privileged concepts above the level of what these concepts "represent" is regarded as possible, then the higher term of the analogy (the *analogatum princeps*)—the transcendent object "signified," although not "represented" in its proper form —must, by virtue of the Thomist theory of knowledge, *be in some way present in us.* If it is not "represented" in us in its proper form, how then is it present to us? How can it be grasped by our thought?[4]

This is an accurate statement of the essence of the problem. Denying that it is possible for us to grasp God purely conceptually—even in the so-called *perfectiones simplices,* or transcendental perfections, our representation remains creaturely—Maréchal asked how we can achieve a real knowledge of God, a knowledge that brings us into contact with him as a reality.

That God is "being" purely and simply and that the creature is "being" and "essence"—what does this mean except that God cannot, properly speaking, be *represented* by any of our objective concepts? For every objective concept marks off the limits of an "essence" (and even implies a representation drawn from sense experience).[5]

The fact that we work with creaturely concepts in our knowledge of God, but consequently subject these concepts continuously to the correction of the *via negationis et eminentiae,* of necessity implies at least a latent comparison between God and the creature.

It is here that we touch the most delicate point of analogical

[4] Maréchal, *Point de départ,* I, 1927[2], 207–208. See also Maréchal, "Le dynamisme intellectuel dans la connaissance objective," *RNP* 29 (1927) 137–165; and *Mélanges J. Maréchal* (Museum Lessianum, Sect. Philos., n. 31), I, Brussels and Paris 1950.

[5] *Point de départ,* V, 1926, 183.

knowledge. We can compare God and the creature in a very real sense, without knowing him directly in himself.[6]

Having established this, Maréchal stated the inescapable dilemma: *either* our knowledge is (as knowledge) dependent on our senses, in which case it cannot be intuitive and is purely notional; *or* our intellectual knowledge is, in one way or another, intuitive, in which case it is (as knowledge) not dependent on our senses.[7] Influenced by Kant's approach to the problem, Maréchal denied the existence of intellectual intuition and consequently, in accordance with Kant's *practical* reason, and probably also under the inspiration of Maurice Blondel, based the real, noetic value of our knowledge of God on an aspect that is not formally noetic, since he denied both intellectual intuition and the ability of purely notional knowledge to come into contact with reality.

We are therefore led to postulate, in our objective knowledge, something other than the static reception and the abstractive analysis of "data." We are constrained to *postulate a movement of thought* which would constantly carry us beyond what is still representable by concepts, to postulate a kind of meta-empirical anticipation which would show us the objective capacity of our intelligence, expanding infinitely until it overcomes all the limitations of being. Apart from that, there is no analogical knowledge of the transcendent. . . . Only an "internal finality" of the intelligence can make it go constantly beyond the present object and seek infinitely a more inclusive object.[8]

The objective and real value of our knowledge of God is

6 *Point de départ*, V, 184.
7 See especially Maréchal, "Abstraction ou Intuition," *RNP* 31 (1929), 27–52, 121–147, and 309–342; or *Mélanges*, I, 102–180.
8 *Point de départ*, V, 185.

thus explained by the dynamism, *not of the content* of our awareness of being, but of the knowing subject. The conceptual is surmounted, not by a non-conceptual, *noetic* contact of the spirit with God, but by the dynamism of the spirit—by my ascertaining that the movement of my spirit again and again goes further than the conceptual content. The dynamic impulse of the spirit is therefore first grasped here, so that the contact with reality makes itself felt *in it*. To recognise the *finitum* as *finitum* means that a comparison is present between the given conceptual content and the limitless character of the impulse of the spirit, which constantly goes beyond the conceptual in the direction of the mystery that is thereby attained but not conceptually grasped. Contained in every knowledge of a creaturely datum there is consequently, as an active experience, an implicit knowledge of God. There is, in the concept, always *more* than the concept itself, more than the conceptual aspect of representation. This is the dynamism of the *voluntas in ratione,* from which the concept arose and through which the intellect moves towards God. The concept is therefore borne up by the dynamism of the spirit and, as a result, projected towards the Infinite. The act of projection, by means of which I rise above the concept and tend towards God, is thus based in the impulse of the spirit, which penetrates the concept, with the result that God is approached, by way of the conceptual content, as the *finis intellectus.*

This is clearly a determined effort to rise above purely notional knowing. The question is, however, whether this does not mark a departure from the standpoint of the intellectual knowledge of God, or whether it does not mean a denial of the strictly noetic value of a real, objective contact with God. The second would, of course, amount to a surrender of a metaphysics of reality. Maréchal, however, considered his thesis to be based on Aquinas's works, and for

this reason it has seemed to me to be profitable to find out
to what extent Aquinas himself accepted an aspect in our
knowledge of God that transcends our concepts, and whether
he looked for this non-conceptual dimension in the dynamism of the spirit or in a certain objective dynamism of the
content of being which is not open to concepts as such. It
may at the same time become clear to what extent the historical teaching of Aquinas differs from the later Thomist
tradition influenced by Scotus.

THE "ACTUS SIGNIFICANDI" TRANSCENDS
THE "RATIO CONCEPTA"

I shall first of all consider the conceptual dimension of our
knowledge of God, in order to see whether, and in what
way, real contact with God goes beyond our concepts.

The Conceptual Dimension of Our
Knowledge of God

Aquinas shows in *ST* I, q. 12, a. 12 how creatures are always
the basis of human knowledge of God, so that all that we can
attain of God is what creatures tell us about him. Aquinas
distinguishes three complementary aspects in this theophany.
In his view, the theophany or creatureliness[9] implies: (1)
the *habitudo Dei ad creaturas,* or, more correctly, the *habitudo creaturarum ad Deum,* which forms the basis of the
via affirmationis; (2) the *differentia creaturarum ab ipso,*
through which God's complete difference from the world
of creatures is affirmed: "he is not of those things which
are caused by him,"[10] with the result that the affirmation

9 In this chapter I am concerned, not to argue the proof of God, but
with the already established proof of God.
10 *ST* I, q. 12, a. 12: "ipse non est aliquid eorum quae ab eo causantur."

is continually corrected by the *via negationis vel remotionis;* and (3) the affirmation of the fullness of being of the divine being-Other: "these things are not separated from him by any deficiency in him, but because he transcends them,"[11] that is, the supreme check on the negative correction of the *via affirmationis* exercised by the *via eminentiae*. This tripartite division is a constant feature in all Aquinas's works,[12] and he summarizes it like this: "We know God . . . as *cause* and by his *transcendence* and by his *utter difference*."[13] These are three inseparable aspects of causality, in which the effect is no different from the act itself of the cause in the other, so that the effect as such is *participativē* the act of the cause itself.[14] *Participatio obiectiva* and *participatio causalis* are thus always essentially connected in Aquinas.[15] The participational character of the effect in respect of its cause consequently implies a *similitudo,* which is naturally accompanied by a basic *dissimilitudo:* "in the effect is found something by means of which it is assimilated to its cause and something by means of which it differs from its cause."[16] Because it is only received, and

---

11 *ST* I, q. 12, a. 12: "haec non removentur ab eo propter eius defectum, sed quia excedit."

12 See, for example: *ST* I, q. 13, a. 1; q. 13, a. 8, ad 2; q. 13, a. 10, ad 5; *BT* q. 6, a. 2 (ed. Marietti 1954, 384); q. 1, a. 2 (322); q. 1, a. 4 (326); *ST* I, q. 84, a. 7, ad 3; *ER* c. 1, lect. 6 (ed. Marietti 1953, 22 *n.* 115); etc.

13 *ST* I, q. 84, a. 7, ad 3: "Deum cognoscimus . . . ut causam et per excessum et per remotionem."

14 *SCG* III, c. 69: "derivatio boni unius in alterum" ("the diverting of the good of one man to another"); *ST* I, q. 62. a. 9, ad 2; *Quodl.* 12, q. 5, a. 1: "participat actum superiorem" ("it participates in the higher act").

15 This accounts for Aquinas's characteristic term *principium efficiens exemplare,* by which the efficiency and the objective participation are expressed *per modum unius.* See *1 Sent.* d. 8, q. 1, a. 3, ad 2; d. 38, q. 1, a. 1; d. 19, q. 5, a. 2; *Verit.* q. 1, a. 8, ad 7; etc.

16 *Potent.* q. 7, a. 5, ad 8: "in effectu invenitur aliquid per quod assimilatur suae causae et aliquid per quod a sua causa differt." The deficiency, however, comes from the creature itself—see *1 Sent.* d. 2, q. 1, a. 2, c.,

thus because of its deficiency, the effect is really distinct from its cause, but not because of what it is positively, since it derives its perfection as such purely from its cause and consequently cannot be *opposed* to it. Assuming this *basis* of distinction, however, the effect is also distinct from its cause in what it is positively. Causality therefore means a single act in two subjects. In the fullest sense, this means *being* the act and, as far as the effect is concerned, *having* or deriving the act.

In the case of creative causality, it is a question of complete dependence. The *aliquid simile* and the *aliquid dissimile* do not point to two partial aspects—they are both total aspects. But this means that the intrinsic nature of the cause, seen from the point of view of the effect, dissolves into mystery. In those texts in which he was free from the influence of Avicenna's essentialism, Aquinas strongly emphasised the fact that the creature is constituted by God according to *existence* and *content* (essence).

From that which is added to the content as its existence, we say that not only is the existence created, but the content itself; for before it has existence, it is nothing, unless perhaps in the intellect of its creator, where it is not a creature, but a creative essence.[17]

---

and especially *ST II–II*, q. 161, a. 3: "In homine duo possunt considerari, scilicet id quod est Dei et id quod est hominis. Hominis autem est quidquid pertinet ad defectum, sed Dei est quidquid pertinet ad salutem et perfectionem" ("Two factors may be considered in man, namely, that which is of God and that which is of man. All that pertains to deficiency is of man, whereas all that pertains to salvation and perfection is of God").

17 *Potent.* q. 3, a. 5, ad 2: "Ex hos ipso quod quidditati esse attribuitur, non solum esse, sed ipsa quidditas creari dicitur: quia antequam esse habeat, nihil est, nisi forte in intellectu creantis, ubi non est creatura, sed creatrix essentia."

I agree with van Boxtel's interpretation of Aquinas,[18] when he says that the *actus essendi* inwardly constitutes the content or essence of Aquinas's later works, so that the act of existence is not seen as a state that has been externally added to something which in itself already possesses intelligible value. The essence is only a definite mode of existence—*this* existence. In this respect, the distinction between *an sit Deus* and *quid sit Deus* is to some extent misleading. The divine existence itself is the supreme intelligible content. This implies that the inability to know the *quid Dei* at the same time and in the same degree includes the inability to know the *existence* of God. Aquinas therefore does not shrink from saying, after the *quinque viae,* that "we cannot know God's existence."[19] The *actus essendi,* which constitutes the *quid Dei,* escapes us. In our natural knowledge of God, we are therefore bound to the dynamism of the world of creatures which reveals God to us, with the result that our terrestrial knowledge of God appears to be more a knowledge of the mysterious intelligibility of the creature than a knowledge of God as such.

It will be quite clear from this that Aquinas unmistakably leaves room for the conceptual aspect in our knowl-

---

[18] J. van Boxtel, "Existentie en waarde in de eerste werken van de H. Thomas van Aquino," *TP* 10 (1948), 221–288; "Existentie en waarde in de latere werken van de H. Thomas van Aquino," *TP* 12 (1950), 59–133; "Metaphysiek van het wezen of metaphysiek van het zijn?", *Verslag Veren. v. Thom.,* Utrecht and Brussels 1951, 1–17. I am of the opinion, however, that the abandonment of essentialism was not a definitive achievement in the historical Thomism, since it is always possible to detect essentialist echoes even in Aquinas's later works, even though these generally occur under the pressure of current philosophical formulae.

[19] *ST* I, q. 3, a. 4, ad 2: "Primo igitur modo accipiendo esse (that is, as the *actus essendi*) non possumus scire esse Dei, *sicut nec* eius essentiam" ("thus in the first sense in which we take existence, we cannot know God's existence, any more than we can know his essence").

edge of God. Because we know God from and in the created world, the conceptual content of this knowledge of God has a bearing on this creaturely reality:

When our intellect knows God from his creatures, for the purpose of understanding God it forms *concepts proportioned to the perfections* which proceed from God to his creatures.[20]

The conceptual representations that are included in our knowledge of God are creaturely, and not concepts of God. Aquinas explicitly draws attention to the fact that, even in and through the supra-predicamental perfections—the *perfectiones simpliciter simplices* of later scholasticism—we possess no real ideas of God. Although these perfections do not, in their content, intrinsically include a limited creaturely mode of being, we nonetheless encounter them only as limited realisations. Conceptually, we cannot imagine these perfections without a definite creaturely mode: "although it is *always* appropriate that the intellect should perceive a creaturely mode in that which is conjointly signified."[21] This means that our intellectual knowledge of God is not possible apart from the conceptual aspect—that our verification of the existence of God of necessity implies a human conceptual aspect. The conceptual representation of, for example, God's goodness is, as a representation, a representation of a creaturely goodness—we have no other conceptual representation. The fact, however, that we can make a significant distinction between the predicamental and the transcendental perfections[22] (although, when we encounter

20 *ST* I, q. 13, a. 4: "Intellectus autem noster cum cognoscat Deum ex creaturis, format ad intelligendum Deum conceptiones proportionatas perfectionibus procedentibus a Deo in creaturas."

21 *1 Sent.* d. 22, q. 1, a. 2, ad 2: "quamvis oporteat in consignificato semper modum creaturae accipere ex parte intellectus."

22 See especially *ST* I, q. 13, a. 3, ad 1; *1 Sent.* d. 22, q. 1, a. 2; *SCG* I, c. 30.

the latter, they are realised only in a creaturely mode, and we can only express them with the *modus creaturae* in which they present themselves to us), makes us aware that in our conceptual awareness something is implied that provides us with an objective perspective onto the *significatum* as this is realised in God.

The "Actus Significandi" and the "Ratio Concepta"

Although Aquinas on the one hand affirms that our knowledge of God includes conceptual aspects, he is on the other hand quite conscious of the fact that knowledge cannot be purely conceptual thought. The texts in which he attempts to define the *similitudo* of the creature to God more precisely are very suggestive in this context. They amount basically to a recognition that our knowledge of the created *similitudo* cannot be defined more precisely in concepts; in other words, that our awareness of it rises above all specifically and even generically defining knowledge expressed in concepts. This is shown *ex professo* in *ST* I, q. 4, a. 3. Accepting as his starting-point the view that causality is a *communicatio propriae perfectionis* by which a single act is realised in two subjects, as giving and as obtained, Aquinas attempts to sound more accurately the depths of our explicit knowledge of the extent of the participation in the effect. In those cases where the *similitudo* goes back to a "sharing in the same *form* of the same *type* and to the same extent,"[23] Aquinas calls the *similitudo* "most perfect" (*perfectissima*), because it points to a conceptual knowledge in which the same content is attributed univocally to different things. In addition, he refers to those cases in which the *similitudo* is

---

23 *ST* I, q. 4, a. 3: "[communicare] in eadem forma secundum eandem rationem et secundum eundem modum."

"a sharing in the same form of the same type, but not to the same extent, but rather to a greater or lesser."[24] This *communicatio formae* points, in Aquinas's view, only to a *similitudo imperfecta,* which he regards as the real basis for a certain form of analogical predication which he calls the "analogy of two (or more) things to a third thing"[25]—that is, the predication of a definite conceptual content to different things on the basis of a "conformity in one thing which is in conformity with the others both before and after."[26] In this case, the *similitudo* is reciprocal. Finally, Aquinas referred to cases of *similitudo* which he is no longer able to define conceptually because they cannot be grasped in specifically or even in generically defined, predicamental concepts. Medieval philosophy spoke here of *causae aequivocae,* where effects derive from a cause that is in an absolute way a *causa prima* at least in a definite sector of being. Aquinas's metaphysics, which was conditioned by the views of antiquity and orientated by cosmology, leads him to distinguish two cases of *similitudo* that cannot be accurately located by conceptual knowledge. In the first of these cases —"sharing the same form, not of the same specific type, but of the same generic likeness"[27]—he refers to sublunary physical events which were regarded in the medieval world as subject to the simultaneous causality of the celestial bodies, the so-called "physical first causes." The likeness between an effect of this kind and its ultimate physical cause is seen by Aquinas to be real, but so minimal that

24 *ST* I, q. 4, a. 3: "[communicare] in eadem forma secundum eandem rationem, sed non secundum eundem modum, sed secundum magis et minus."

25 *ST* I, q. 4, a. 3: "analogia duorum (vel plurium) ad aliquid tertium."

26 *ST* I, q. 4, a. 3: "convenientia in aliquo uno quod eis per prius et posterius convenit." See also *I Sent.* d. 35, q. 1, a. 4 (ed. Mandonnet, 820).

27 *ST* I, q. 4, a. 3: "[communicare in eadem forma] non secundum eandem rationem speciei [sed secundum eandem similitudinem generis]."

our conceptual knowledge is only able to provide a generic description of it. I have only quoted this medieval example in order to situate the last case of *similitudo* more clearly. This is the *similitudo* of the creature to God—the "likeness" that has its origins in God's complete and absolute causality. Aquinas does not call it a participation in the form of the same type, species or genus; it is said to be "a participation according to a certain kind of analogy."[28] In this case Aquinas regards the *similitudo* not only as not reciprocal,[29] but also, though real, as "very slight."[30] It is, in his opinion, such that not only is it impossible to grasp it in specifically defined concepts, but it escapes even the final, minimal possibility of abstract understanding—generic definition. Aquinas means by this that it is not conceivable in concepts, that it cannot be understood or grasped conceptually:

A creature represents God and is similar to him insofar as it possesses a certain perfection; not however in such a manner that it represents him as something of the same species or genus, but rather as a surpassing principle, whose form the effects fall short of, but nevertheless with which the effects attain a certain likeness.[31]

Aquinas therefore affirms on the one hand that we know

28 *ST* I, q. 4, a. 3: "[participatio] formae . . . secundum eandem rationem speciei vel generis, sed secundum aliqualem analogiam."

29 See *ST* I, q. 4, a. 3, ad 4: "Nullo modo concedendum est quod Deus sit similis creaturae" ("in no way may we concede that God is similar to his creature"). See also the same doctrine in *1 Sent.* d. 35, q. 1, a. 4, ad 6 (ed. Mandonnet, 821).

30 *Verit.* q. 2, a. 3, ad 9: "similitudo realis, sed minima."

31 *ST* I, q. 13, a. 2: "Quaelibet creatura in tantum Eum repraesentat et est Ei similis, in quantum perfectionem aliquam habet; non tamen ita quod repraesentet Eum sicut aliquid eiusdem speciei vel generis, sed sicut excellens principium, a cuius forma effectus deficiunt, cuius tamen aliqualem similitudinem effectus consequuntur."

that a likeness exists between the creature and God, and on the other hand that this creaturely likeness escapes the grasp of our specific, and even of our merely generic, conceptual knowledge. It is, in his view, impossible to grasp this *similitudo* conceptually. The importance of this affirmation is that it is precisely *this* similitude (as the essential aspect of dependence on God or absolute participation) which, according to Aquinas, forms the basis of the objective value of our knowledge of God. The really existing *similitudo* of the creature to God is therefore an immanent *beyond* of our predicamental and conceptual knowledge. It is an intellectual content which is, however, at the same time not confined by any specific and generic limitations. The "likeness" of the creature to its creator is not a *"definite* proportion or measure,"´ because, though there is a real likeness, the *dissimilitudo* is infinitely great and God is incomparable.[32] All our representations of God derived from the created world can certainly *signify* God, "but not definitively or exhaustively."[33] In other words, we have no adequate *ratio* of God's perfection—we have no proper concepts of God. "No creature has such a relationship to God that by it he is able to give content to the divine perfection."[34] In view of the fact that our speaking about God is only the verbal expression or putting into words of the conceptual ideas that we derive from our knowledge of creatures, the *ratio nominis* or the conceptual content goes back directly to the creature. The *res significata per nomen* transcends the *res ut concepta* (or the *ratio nominis* or the *significatio nominis*). Nowhere does Aquinas assert that the *significatio*

[32] *DN* c. 9, lect. 3 (ed. Marietti 1950, 312): "determinata proportio seu mensura."

[33] *Potent.* q. 7, a. 5, ad 9: "sed non definitive vel circumscriptive."

[34] *Verit.* q. 2, a. 11: "Nulla creatura habet talem habitudinem ad Deum per quam possit divina perfectio determinari."

transcends the *repraesentatio,* because, with him, *significatio* always means the conceptual content. But the reality signified or referred to transcends the conceptual content:

The reality signified transcends the conceptual content of the name.[35] These names [that is, those which are used absolutely of God, although their constant point of support for our knowledge is in the creature] are not used to signify these processes . . . but to signify the very principle of things, just as in him life pre-exists, though in a more excellent manner than we can understand or signify.[36]

The absolute names of God signify or refer to God in himself, but via the intermediary signification of the conceptual content derived from the creature. "The reality is signified by the name [or term] via the concept or content, i.e., via the signification [that is, conceptual content] of the name [or term]."[37] The *res significata* and the *res concepta* were not simply identical in historical Thomism. The *act of signifying* goes further than the *ratio nominis,* but it exceeds this *ratio* in the direction indicated by its content itself, in such a way that the reality is really envisaged, but not conceptually grasped. The fact that this act of signifying goes further than the conceptual representation was seen by Aquinas to be based on the creature's natural, objective pointing to God, although this objective tendency escapes our precise conceptual definition. Even though we therefore cannot really abstract the creaturely mode of the so-called

35 *ST* I, q. 13, a. 5: "Res significata excedit significationem nominis."

36 *ST* I, q. 13, a. 2, ad 2: "Haec nomina non imponuntur ad significandum ipsos processus, . . . sed ad significandum ipsum rerum principium, prout in eo praeexistit vita, licet eminentiori modo quam intelligatur vel significetur."

37 "Res significatur per nomen mediante conceptione seu ratione, i.e. per nominis significationem." This is the fundamental doctrine of the whole of *ST* I, q. 13; see a. 4, ad 1 and a. 1.

transcendental perfections from their deepest inner meaning
—with the result that we cannot attribute this mode and
this concept to God—it would nonetheless seem that Aquinas was affirming that we do not surrender the entire content of knowledge with our denial of the creaturely mode
of these perfections (which we furthermore know only as
realised creaturally). Our real knowledge of God, however,
cannot be a purely explicit or conceptual knowledge.

There is, moreover, a certain fluctuation in Aquinas's
statements. In some places, he called the *ratio nominis* or the
conceptually represented content the basis of our affirmative *nomina divina*.[38] In other places, however, he situated
the *ratio nominis* on the side of the *modus significandi* and
the *impositio nominis (ex creaturis)*: *"Res* nominis (de
Deo et creaturis dicti) per prius est in Deo secundum suum
modum; sed *ratio* nominis per posterius."*[39] The latter is
more in keeping with Aquinas's constant doctrine that we
have no real concepts of God and that the representations
with which we work in our explicit knowledge of God are
creaturely representations. In any event, *ratio nominis* always means the *conceptual* content in his case, and this
always goes back to the creatural perfections. This means
that the *ratio nominis* as the conceptual content cannot be
identified with the noetic encounter with the *significatum*.
These differing statements (on the one hand, "ratio nominis
per posterius est in Deo" and, on the other, "ratio nominis

---

[38] In Thomas's view, there was, in the *content* of our awareness, as far
as the so-called transcendental perfections are concerned, something that we
predicate *proprie* of God and even *per prius* (I, q. 13, a. 3), at least "quantum ad rem significatam, licet non quantum ad modum significandi" *(In
1 Sent.* d. 22, q. 1, a. 2). Thomas consequently maintained, like the *Graeci,*
that even these perfections could be both denied of God and affirmed. In
SCG I, c. 30 fin., he elucidated this claim thus: "affirmari quidem propter
nominis rationem; negari vero propter significandi modum."

[39] *SCG* I, 34.

. . . *per prius* [est] in Deo") are clearly reconciled in the
Scriptum: "Illa *ratio* . . . per prius in Deo, per posterius in
creaturis *existens*."[40] The word *existens* here shows that
ratio should be interpreted in this context not formally as
ratio or the conceptually represented content of knowledge,
but as the realised content. "Ratio . . . existens" in this
context therefore refers to the "res *significata* per rationem."
This shows that, in Aquinas's view, the transcendental perfections retain their full transcendental character only if
they are not simply regarded as *ratio,* since they must then
of necessity be situated among the predicamental perfections and cannot consequently, as conceptual content, be
"per prius de Deo dicta." We are thus confronted with the
problem as stated by Maréchal, that a conceptual content
as such can never be ascribed to God—the *conceptual* content of "goodness" is a representation of creaturely goodness.
And yet Aquinas did call God formally and absolutely
good. The divine mode of goodness escapes our conceptual
representation, but this mode *is* God himself and not, so
to speak, a mode added to the creaturely representation of
goodness. It is also not creaturely goodness from which we
would actually have succeeded in eliminating the creaturely
mode so that a concept of "divine goodness," purified to
the utmost degree, would be left to us. ". . . Oporte(a)t in
consignificato *semper* modum creaturae accipere ex parte
intellectus."[41] There must therefore be more than purely
conceptual knowledge. Simply notional knowledge seemed
to Aquinas to lead only to agnosticism because, after com-
pleting the *via negationis et eminentiae,* the conceptual content of our divine names still continues to be creaturely. We
are not left with a *ratio* in which the creaturely mode is
absent or, in the Scotist view, neutral with respect to a

40 *In 1 Sent.* d. 22, q. 1, a. 2, ad 3.
41 *In 1 Sent.* d. 22, q. 1, a. 2, ad 2.

limited or unlimited possibility of realisation. The concept
as such is still a creaturely concept. "Ut sic post omne quod
intellectus noster ex creaturis manuductus de Deo *concipere*
potest, hoc ipsum quod Deus est remaneat occultum et
ignotum. Non solum enim Deus non est lapis aut sol, . . .
sed nec est talis vita aut essentia, *qualis* ab intellectu nostro
concipi potest; et sic hoc ipsum quod Deus est, cum excedat
omne illud quod a nobis *apprehenditur,* nobis remanet ignotum."[42]

This accounts for Aquinas's "agnostic" statements at the
purely notional level: "Manifestum est enim quod hoc
nomen 'bonum,' cum sit a nobis impositum, non signat *nisi
quod nos mente capimus.* Unde, cum Deus sit supra mentem
nostram, super excedit hoc nomen."[43] Again and again,
whenever he asked what we really know of God, Aquinas
gave the same answer—firstly, "quid non est" and then,
in immediate association with this, "qualiter alia se habent
ad ipsum."[44] In other words, the *modus divinus* of a perfection can only be *negatively* and *relatively* situated. This
would seem at first sight to be rather dubious and to bring

[42] *DN* Prol. (ed. Marietti 1950, 1). This dictum is not simply a neutral
commentary on a text which is alien to Thomas, but the expression of the
entire treatise *De Divinis Nominibus,* as condensed by Thomas in I, q. 13.

[43] *DN* c. 13, lect. 3 (ed. Marietti 1950, 369). See also *In 1 Sent.* d. 8, q.
1, a. 1, ad 4; *SCG* I, c. 5 and 14; III, c. 49; IV, c. 1; *Verit.* q. 2, a. 1, ad
9; *Potent.* q. 7, a. 5, ad 14; *BT* q. 1, a. 2, ad 1; q. 1, a. 4, ad 10; *DN* c. 1,
lect. 3; c. 2, lect. 4; c. 7, lect. 4, c. fin.; c. 13, lect. 3; this also applies to the
conceptual character of supernatural and even mystical knowledge of God
(see, for example, II-II, q. 8, a. 7). Thomas's preference for the *via negativa*
can therefore not be denied; see *SCG* I, c. 14: "est autem via remotionis
utendum praecipue in consideratione divinae substantiae" and especially
DN c. 1, lect. 3: "hoc enim est ultimum ad quod pertingere possumus
circa cognitionem divinam in hac vita, quod Deus est supra id quod a
nobis cogitare potest; et ideo nominatio Dei quae est per remotionem est
maxime propria" (ed. Marietti 1950, 28).

[44] Or in similar terms—the "an est" and the "quod causa aliorum est"
of *SCG* I, c. 30; II, c. 49.

Aquinas dangerously close to the position taken up by Maimonides or even the modernists. We should, however, not play these statements off against the fundamental affirmations of I, q. 13, a. 2 and a. 3, in which Aquinas traced some divine names back not to a negative or relative knowledge, but to an absolute, real, objective and positive knowledge of God which, however, as such, while using concepts, transcends the conceptual. "Intellectus negationis semper fundatur in aliqua affirmatione."[45] The content of the so-called transcendental perfections objectively indicates the perspective in which God is to be found—we have a sense of God positively at the end of, but nonetheless within, the *transcendentalia*. He is certainly supra-predicamental, but not "supra-transcendental." What we have here is a positive intellectual content that *directs* us *objectively* towards God's own mode of being. Our so-called "concepts of God" really define an intelligible content that is, however, *open* to the mystery. The typically noetic value of our knowledge of God is therefore situated in a projective act, in which we *reach out for* God, but do not grasp him in understanding, although we are well aware that he is to be found in the precise *direction* in which we are reaching. By this we mean that our knowledge of God is not simply a blind shot in the dark. God is really to be found *within* the perspective of the intelligible content of the *transcendentalia*, which therefore really refer us positively to God. We cannot, however, positively situate him more accurately within this *definite*, noetically referential perspective. If we wish to do this, we are thrown back on what Aquinas called the negative and relative knowledge, that is, the "quid non est" and the "qualiter alia se habent ad ipsum."

Summing up Aquinas's view of this problem, then, we

45 *Potent.* q. 7, a. 5.

must say that we know God positively, but that we cannot
form any conceptual representation in our minds of God's
own mode of being, the *modus eminentiae*. To this end, we
can only appeal to *nomina negativa* and *relativa*. That is to
say that our *conceptual* representation is negative and relative (because it is creaturely), but as the *expression* of a
positive and affirmative content which, however, remains,
by definition, unexpressed and implicit. It is, however, precisely this implicit content which allows us to use negative
and relative divine names. "Unde, nisi intellectus humanus
aliquid de Deo affirmative cognosceret, nihil de Deo posset
negare."[46] Our proper-but-negative and our positive-but-
improper knowledge of God is therefore borne up by a
proper-and-positive knowledge of him which, however, remains *unexpressed*, but does form the matrix of the conceptual aspects in our knowledge of God.

The foregoing has shown that there are, according to
Aquinas's doctrine, conceptual aspects in our knowledge of
God, although we do not *grasp* God notionally. If we nonetheless speak of coming into contact with God in our knowledge, then we base this on the objective *perspective* that is
distinctive to the contents themselves of our knowledge.[47]
In this way, Aquinas avoided both agnosticism, symbolism
or pragmatism and all forms of anthropomorphism. The
possibility of aiming at God, in a confused but objective
way, is a result of the fact that the reality in which we live
is a divine creation and, as such, thus from an inner dynamism, revelatory of God. Aquinas avoided agnosticism by
affirming that God is not *outside* the *transcendentalia*, and
that there is "something" in creatures which is also to be

[46] *Potent.* q. 7, a. 5; see also *SCG* I, c. 25; III, c. 2; I–II, q. 72, a. 6;
In 1 Sent. d. 35, q. 1, a. 1, ad 2.
[47] *DN* I, lect. 2: we reach out beyond the concepts.

found in God, but which we cannot express. God is really good, in himself, but we always have a creaturely representation of goodness. For us, it is a definite goodness, the definite character of which can never entirely disappear even in a confused expression of "goodness as such." For this reason, the *modus divinus* of God's goodness—God himself—cannot be conceptually grasped. We therefore really *signify* the *substantia Dei* on the basis of the *objective dynamism* of the *content* of the so-called *trancendentalia*, that is, on the basis of what in reality objectively refers, beyond the limits of the finite, to God. That is why Aquinas frequently spoke of the *virtus essendi,* so as to emphasise even more strongly the objective dynamism of the *actus essendi* that is offered to us in the finite. The speculative and objective value of our knowledge of God is therefore to be found in an act of *tending towards,* with the result that we do not *properly* attribute concepts to God (we do not *attribuere Deo*), but, in the direct line of these contents, we do *tend towards* God (we do *tendere in Deum*). Because of their own content, the so-called *transcendentalia* refer noetically to the intelligibility of God, which we nonetheless do not grasp conceptually. Our knowledge of God thus possesses a speculative value—although it cannot be grasped in concepts, it is still a true, definite and meaningful knowledge. This does not mean that it can manage without concepts. Thomas expressed these two aspects—the conceptual and the non-conceptual—of our knowledge of God thus: "Huiusmodi quidem nomina significant substantiam divinam et praedicantur de Deo substantialiter, sed deficiunt a repraesentatione ipsius."[48] One result of this is also that the more precise expression of the exact content of our

48 I, q. 13, a. 2.

knowledge of God always involves a certain confusion—
we know the *quid Dei* only *sub quadam confusione*.[49] It is
a *quantulacumque cognitio*,[50] a noetic tending towards God,
from a creaturely, excentric standpoint. It is the *intellectual*
character of our knowledge of God that is manifested in
this tending towards which is non-conceptual, but nonetheless linked to concepts. "Anima vero, quia extremum
gradum in intellectualibus tenet, participat naturam intel-
lectualem magis defective quasi obumbrata."[51] This noetic
structure permits only of an "intellectualis quidam intui-
tus"[52] of God, that is, it allows us to be aware of an objective perspective in our knowledge, to know that God is
present in the definite direction that is indicated by the conceptual content itself, and in no other direction.

It is clear that, whenever Aquinas mentioned "dynamism," he always had an *objective* dynamism in mind. It
is certainly not without good reason that we make a distinction between the so-called transcendental perfections
and the predicamental perfections, even though we see the
transcendentalia only as finitely realised. For we make this
distinction not because of the imperfection of our knowledge, but because of the content itself, which is offered
objectively as transcendental. This structure of our knowledge of God is even more clearly confirmed by Thomas's
doctrine of the so-called analogy of God.

AQUINAS'S ANALOGY OF GOD AND CREATURES

It is well known that, in Aristotle, *analogia* referred exclusively to a *proportionalitas*, a term which was originally

49 *BT* q. 6. a. 3.
50 *In 4 Sent.* d. 49, q. 2, a. 7, ad 7.
51 *In 2 Sent.* d. 13, q. 1, a. 6 (p. 104).
52 *SCG* IV, c. 1.

borrowed from geometrical and arithmetical relationships and then applied to qualitative relationships.[53] On the other hand, however, it is also a fact that what Thomas called formally "analogical" was never called analogical by Aristotle, that is, homonymous predication on the basis of a relationship—the so-called *ta pros ti* and the *ta aph'henos,* the *per prius et per posterius dicta.* In an analytical study, H. A. Wolfson[54] has shown that, because of the new term *amphibolos,* used by Alexander of Aphrodisias to denote the Aristotelian "homonymous prediction on the basis of a *proportio,*" the term *analogikos* eventually came, after many fluctuations in the Arabic terminology for Alexander's *amphibolos,* to mean precisely that class of expression that was never called "analogical" by Aristotle himself, that is, the *per prius et per posterius dicta.* It is also characteristic that, as the examples classified by Wolfson show, *analogon* was never used in this Arabic and Jewish philosophy in Cajetan's sense of an ontological *proportionalitas* or of an analogy between different substances, but only in the sense of an analogy *per prius et per posterius—ens,* as said of the *accidens,* the *substantia,* creatures and God. I do not propose, however, to go any further here into this finding, which is in itself very instructive, namely that the analogy of being was seen in Arabic metaphysics essentially as a predication *per prius et per posterius,* a predication on the basis of a relationship.

The term *analogon* is also to be found in the more neo-Platonic, Dionysian scholasticism of the twelfth and the early thirteenth centuries, used formally as a *per prius et*

53 See. G. L. Muskens, *De vocis "analogias" significatione ac usu apud Aristotelem,* Groningen 1943; "Aristoteles en het probleem der *analogia entis,*" *Studia Catholica* 21 (1946), 72–86.
54 "The amphibolous Terms in Aristotle, Arabic Philosophy and Maimonides," *Harvard Theological Review* 31 (1938), 151–173.

per posterius dictum.[55] In Alexander of Hales' fully worked
out teaching on analogy and in the doctrines of William
of Middleton included in Alexander's work, the term *analogia* is also encountered with the evident meaning of a
"predication on the basis of a relationship between one
thing and another." In other words, an analogical predication is a predication in which one name, which is, so to
speak, the proper name of a definite thing, is also applied
to other things, because these things bear a certain relationship to that one thing. The name of the one thing is
therefore *transferred* to the other, and thus predicated
per posterius, of the other as well, leaving the question un-
decided as to whether the *ratio nominis* is or is not inherent
in the other subjects named. *Analogice* is therefore simply
equivalent to *secundum prius et posterius*—"per posterius
et ita analogice" or "analogice, hoc est: secundum prius
et posterius."[56]

On the basis of these few historical premises, a certain
vigilance in the study of Aquinas's analogy of God is certainly not out of place. Did Aquinas remain within this
historical framework, or did he deviate from it in the direction taken later by Cajetan?

In my opinion, Aquinas used the word analogy in a double sense, the first meaning being the basis of the second.
He borrowed *analogia* in the sense of a material relationship from Aristotle, who did not use it as a "predication"
or *nominatio,* that is, as intermediate between a univocal
and an equivocal saying, but rather to denote an objective

---

[55] See certain suggestive data in E. Schenkler, *Die Lehre von den gött-
lichen Namen in der Summa Alexanders von Hales. Ihre Prinzipien und
ihre Methode* (Freiburger Theologische Studien XLVI), Freiburg 1938.

[56] *Summa Alexandrina,* P. II, inq. 2, tr. 1, q. 3, c. 1 (ed. Quaracchi, t.
I, n. 366, p. 544); *op. cit.,* q. 1, a. 3 (I, n. 347, p. 514); Tract. introd., q.
2, m. 3, c. 2 (I, n. 21, p. 32); also I, n. 347, pp. 514–515; n. 366, pp. 542–
544; n. 388–389, pp. 572–574; n. 295, pp. 416 and 418; t. II, n. 485, p. 673.

relationship (in fact, a proportional relationship), forming the basis for a definite kind of homonymous predication or similarity of name. Aquinas too regarded *analogia* in the first place as an objective or ontological relationship (the nature of which will shortly become apparent). In addition, however, he also called the unity of predication, on the basis of this objective *analogia*, an *analogical predication*, thus forming the intermediate between univocity and complete equivocity. An example of this objective and real analogy can be found in I, q. 4, a. 3. This offers the real basis for an "analogical predication" in the logical and verbal or the grammatical and philosophical sense, as described in I, q. 13, a. 5. Both are, of course, closely related, as the analogical predication implies a unity of predication or similarity of name on the basis of a real analogy or *proportio*.

The Real Analogia of the Creature to God

As far as I have been able to ascertain, there were three distinct stages in Aquinas's teaching about the ontological analogy of God. The first stage, up to 1256 (the date of the first two books of the *Scriptum*), was followed by a short intermediary period, roughly between 1256 and 1257. After a beginning had been made in the third and fourth books of the *Scriptum*, this second stage reached a temporary peak in a few questions in *De veritate* and was finally followed by the third period. It is this final stage, already initiated in the remaining questions of *De veritate*, which provides us with Thomas's definitive view.

1. When Thomas spoke, in the first three books of his commentary on the *Sententiae*, about the real relationship of the creature to the Creator, he never referred to this relationship with the term *proportionalitas*, but always with

the term *proportio unius ad alterum*. The term *proportionalitas* appears to have been used in these books only to denote proportions which offer a basis for a metaphorical manner of speaking,[57] and thus also possibly for metaphors relating to God. Thomas refused, however, to take a *similitudo proportionalitatis* of this kind as the basis for our real true knowledge of God. For him, the real basis of this knowledge was the *analogia creaturae ad Creatorem*,[58] that is, the "communitas ... ex eo quod unum esse et rationem ab altero recipit ...; creatura enim non habet esse nisi secundum quod a primo ente descendit" (*loc. cit.*). The real analogy here is a *similitudo imitationis* or a *proportio unius ad alterum*, in which the *similitudo* is thus not reciprocal.[59] Thomas threw more light on this analogy by contrasting it with a second case of "analogical predication on a real basis," that is, with the case in which the subjects referred to display a reciprocal likeness. He called this relationship a "proportio *plurium* ad aliquid unum," and described it later in the *Summa* as a "convenientia in eadem forma, secundum eandem rationem sed non secundum eundem modum, sed secundum magis et minus."[60] But the analogy with reference to God was, for Aquinas, a likeness of imitation without reciprocation, a *proportio unius ad alterum*.

[57] See, for example, *In 1 Sent.* d. 22, q. 1, a. 2, ad 3 (p. 536); d. 34, q. 3, a. 1, ad 2 (p. 798); d. 45, q. 1, a. 4 (p. 1039); *In 2 Sent.* d. 16, q. 1, a. 2, ad 5 (p. 401); see also in the third and fourth books, *In 3 Sent.* d. 2, q. 1, a. 1, sol. 1, ad 3 (pp. 56–57); *In 4 Sent.* d. 1, q. 1, sol. 5, ad 3 (p. 16). The following text, from *In 2 Sent.* d. 13, q. 1, a. 2 (p. 330), is also characteristic: "Transferuntur corporalia in spiritualibus per quandam similitudinem; quae quidem est similitudo proportionabilitatis; et hanc similitudinem oportet *reducere* in aliquam communitatem univocationis vel analogiae." The basis of the *proportionalitas* is univocity, that is, the *proportio;* see later.

[58] *In 1 Sent.* Prol., q. 1, a. 2, ad 2 (p. 10).

[59] *In 1 Sent.* d. 35, q. 1, a. 4, ad 6 (p. 821); see *op. cit.*, in c. (p. 820).

[60] I, q. 4, a. 3.

It is true that he spoke of "una *ratio* (sapientiae) secundum analogiam,"[61] but we should not be misled by this reference to *una ratio*. There are, after all, two kinds of *unitas rationis secundum analogiam*—"Quaedam secundum convenientiam in aliquo uno quod eis per prius et posterius convenit; et haec analogia non potest esse inter Deum et creaturam ...; alia analogia est, secundum quod unum imitatur aliud quantum potest nec perfecte ipsum assequitur; et haec analogia est creaturae ad Deum."[62] The first analogy (the analogy which embraces both analogates as in an "accolade") consists of the realisation of the "same *ratio*" in different subjects, but *secundum magis et minus*. According to this analogy, both mortal and venial sin, for example, were regarded by Aquinas as really "sins."[63] The analogy of God, on the other hand, permits of no "accolade"—the unity of the *ratio nominis* in the similarity of the name is not caused by the abstract character of that particular *ratio*, as if this *ratio* were to abstract from the real differences, but by the *unity of a concrete reality*. In medieval terms, this was expressed in the following way. The unity of the *ratio nominis* is based on the unity of a concrete, ontologically realised *ratio*, to which other realities are really in proportion, with the result that, as far as naming is concerned, the name of that concrete reality, indicated in and through the *ratio nominis*, also enters into the naming of the other subjects, and does this on a basis of this material relationship. The *una ratio* therefore does not refer to an abstract *communitas*, but to the unity of the concrete reality, to an *una numero*. "Dicendum quod inter Deum et creaturam *non* est similitudo per *convenientiam in*

---

61 *In 1 Sent.* d. 22, q. 1, a. 2, ad 3 (p. 536).
62 *In 1 Sent.* d. 35, q. 1, a. 4, in c. (p. 820); compare this with I, q. 4, a. 3.
63 *In 2 Sent.* d. 42, q. 1, a. 3 (p. 1057).

aliquo uno communi, sed per imitationem."[64] The basis
of the similarity of names here is the "absolute participation" of the creature, "secundum analogiam tantum, *prout*
scilicet Deus est ens per essentiam et alia per participa-
tionem," as it was to be expressed later in the *Summa*.[65]
"Creatura enim non habet esse nisi secundum quod a primo
ente descendit."[66] No mention was made anywhere in these
books to the *analogia proportionalitatis* in the context of the
analogy of God, except in connection with the divine
metaphors.

2. This was followed by a sudden change, at least in Aquinas's terminology. In *In 3 Sent*. d. 1, q. 1, a. 1, ad 3 (p. 10)
and *In 4 Sent*. d. 49, q. 2, a. 1, ad 6 (ed. Parmae, p. 1200),
he no longer calls the relationship between the creature and
God a *proportio*, but refers to it as a *proportionalitas*. This
is even more explicit in *De veritate* q. 2, a. 3, ad 4; a. 11, ad
2, ad 4 and ad 6; q. 8, a. 1, ad 6 and q. 23, a. 7, ad 9. After
this, Aquinas just as suddenly ceased to use the term *proportionalitas* in connection with the analogy of God.

The commentators in the line of Cajetan, however, had
recourse to these texts. According to them, we have to do
with *una ratio abstracta* which possesses, by virtue of its
supreme universality, "transcendental predicability"—one
definition is, in this view, predicable of all subjects, not in
a univocal manner, but in a proportionally unified manner.
The *transcendentalia* are, according to this view, *concepts*
which owe their conceptual unity to the fact that, in the
ratio abstracta, the real differences are present only in a
confused manner. According to this thesis, then, we have
concepts that actually include both the creaturely and the

[64] *In 1 Sent*. d. 35, q. 1, a. 4, ad 6 (p. 821).
[65] I, q. 4, a. 3, ad 3.
[66] *In 1 Sent*. Prol., q. 1, a. 2, ad 2 (p. 10).

divine reality, but in such a way that these differences are
not expressed.

This solution of the later Thomistic commentators was
clearly influenced by the Scotist view. According to Scotus,
we do indeed know God only *ex creaturis,* but this is not
the same as *in creaturis.* Conceptually, we have a positive
knowledge of the being itself of God. The *transcendentalia*
are true and therefore univocal concepts, which abstract
from the mode of finiteness and infiniteness. We are therefore able to conceive their *ratio formalis* in itself, apart
from their more precise determinations.[67] In itself, the formal
ratio of goodness, truth, etc., pertains univocally both to God
and to creatures, so that we have a positive *concept* of God
as *being,* by means of which we *grasp* him conceptually.
"Omnis inquisitio de Deo supponit habere conceptum eundem univocum quem accipit ex creaturis."[68] This is the
point of view of essentialism consistently carried through.
Really, God and the creature have nothing in common,
and yet we have concepts that point to a *ratio formalis*
that is common to both: "Deus et creatura non sunt primo
diversa in *conceptibus*; tamen sunt primo diversa in *realitate,* quia in nulla realitate conveniunt."[69] The concept
"being," "good," "true," etc., applied to God, differs from
the same concept, applied to the creature, not by the addition of a specific *differentia,* but simply according to a
modus. The difference is to be found in a "distinctio *reali-
tatis* et *modi* proprii et intrinseci eiusdem,"[70] in a distinction between the concept of the same real quiddity (present
in both subjects) and its more or less perfect mode. In this
sense, no single concept is really a specific concept of God,

---

67 *In 1 Sent.* d. 3, q. 1, a. 4, n. 6 (Opus Oxiense, t. 1, 309–310).
68 *Op. cit.* n. 10 (t. I, p. 312).
69 *In 1 Sent.* d. 8, q. 3, a. 1, n. 11 (t. I, p. 598).
70 *In 1 Sent.* d. 8, q. 3, a. 3, n. 27 (t. I, p. 614).

since the so-called transcendental concepts make an abstraction from both the divine and the creaturely mode. But although they neither include nor exclude both these modes, we do reach, in this *ratio formalis communis*, something of God himself in a purely notional manner.[71]

The influence of Scotus on the solution of Cajetan and his followers can already be ascertained in the problem of the distinction between the divine attributes. According to Scotus, the *ratio formalis* of goodness was not the *ratio formalis* of wisdom, in view of the fact that there was always a formal non-identity whenever the *ratio formalis* of different perfections was irreducible. As a formal *ratio*, wisdom is consequently not goodness. But wisdom and goodness are really present in God. As wisdom in God, this *ratio* is present as wisdom and not as goodness. God's real wisdom is formally not his real goodness. Since, however, both are present in God, they are consequently present as formally distinct. God's simplicity is nonetheless saved, and this is achieved by virtue of the *infinitas* of each of these *rationes formales* that are present in God. Because infiniteness is the divine mode of this particular *ratio formalis*, *infinitas*— which is not a divine attribute, but the divine mode of all the divine attributes—is the reason for the ontological identity of divine wisdom and divine goodness, even though the *rationes formales* remain formally and really distinct.[72] God's

---

[71] See C. L. Shircel, *The Univocity of the Concept of Being in the Philosophy of Duns Scotus*, Washington 1942; T. Barth, *De fundamento univocitatis apud Joh. D. Scotus*, Rome 1939; E. Gilson, "Avicenne et le point de départ de Duns Scot," *Arch. d'Hist. Doctr. Litt. du M.A.* 2 (1927), 89–151; "L'objet de la métaphysique selon Duns Scot," *Mediaeval Studies* 10 (1948), 72–92; "Simplicité divine et attributs divins selon Duns Scot," *Arch. d'Hist. Doctr. Litt. du M.A.* 24 (1949), 9–43. These articles by Gilson have been collected in his *Jean Duns Scot. Introduction à ses positions fondamentales* (Etudes de philosophie médiévale, Vol. XLII), Paris 1952.

[72] *In 1 Sent.* d. 8, q. 4, a. 3, n. 26 (t. I, p. 639), n. 17 (t. I, p. 633), n. 18 (t. I, pp. 633–634).

wisdom is his goodness, but that which is God's wisdom
is not that which is his goodness.

Many Thomist commentators, influenced by these ideas,
have claimed that there is a foundation in God for the
assignation of divine attributes to him in a distinct manner
and, for this reason, they speak of a *distinctio virtualis minor*
in God himself. Thomas, however, denied in the most em-
phatic way that there was any foundation in God for the
assignation of all these attributes to him *in a distinct manner.* He did say that there was a real foundation in God for
the designation of God's being in and through the *transcendentalia* ("omnes istae multae rationes et diversae *habent aliquid correspondens* in ipso Deo, cuius omnes istae
conceptiones intellectus sunt similitudines"),[73] but denied
that there was any foundation *in him* for the assignation
of these perfections to him in a distinct manner. It is only
in creatures, as the point of departure for our knowledge
of God, that a real foundation can be found for the distinction of concepts. "Diversitatis ergo vel multiplicitatis nominum causa est ex parte intellectus nostri." (*loc. cit.*) Thomas
thus did not deny the reality of intellect, will, goodness
and wisdom in God, but he did deny the reality or even the
"virtuality" of the *distinction* in God—"non secundum rem,
sed secundum rationem."[74] We must blame the limited nature of our knowledge for the fact that we cannot formally
call wisdom goodness. Thomas's position in this is therefore
diametrically opposed to Scotus's and the Thomist solutions
inspired by Scotus: "quia cum singula nomina *determinate*
aliquid significant *distinctum* ab aliis, venientia in divinam
praedicationem, non significant illud finite, sed infinite; sicut
nomen sapientiae *prout in rebus creatis* accipitur significat
aliquid distinctum a iustitia; . . . sed cum in divinis accipitur

[73] *Potent.* q. 7, a. 6.
[74] I, q. 28, a. 2.

non significat aliquid determinatum ad genus et ad speciem seu distinctionem ab aliis perfectionibus, sed aliquid infinitum."[75] Thomas was not in any way denying here that there was a distinction between the different attributes precisely as concepts. What he was saying was that the act of predication was directed towards a *non finitum*, a reality that cannot be grasped conceptually. This means that we work, with regard to God, only with natural concepts, in which the notional representation is of its very nature creaturely (and thus includes multiplicity and distinction). It does not, however, mean that we attribute the concept as such to God, but that we know that God is, as it were, situated in the extension of this concept. The metaphysical problem was, however, basically altered in the work of Duns Scotus, who forms the link between Aquinas and later Thomism, and this has resulted in the obscuring of the distinctive character of Aquinas's teaching about the analogy of God. That is why it is important to find out the precise meaning of Aquinas's shift of attention from the *proportio* to the *proportionalitas*—a change which, by the way, was only temporary.

In *In 4 Sent.* d. 49, q. 2, a. 1, ad 6 (ed. Parmae, p. 1200), Aquinas in fact disclaimed his earlier view that a *similitudo secundum proportionem* existed between the creature and God. In considering this question, however, the context must be kept firmly in mind. By *proportio* Thomas meant, in this context, a *measurable* relationship: "proportio *determinata.*" In view of the fact that the distance between God and creature cannot be measured, there could be no question of a *proportio*, although Thomas admitted that *proportio* could certainly also have a wider meaning, and could denote unmeasurable relationships as well.[76] But in

75 *DN* I, lect. 3 (ed. Marietti, 1950, p. 31).
76 *In 4 Sent.* d. 49, q. 2, a. 1, ad 6 (ed. Parmae, p. 1200).

its strict sense, the *proportio* included a *certitudo mensurationis*, whereas the *proportio ordinis*, that is, *secundum proportionalitatem*, abstracted from the determination of the distances.[77] Because of the infinite and therefore unmeasurable distance between God and the creature, Thomas preferred to use the term *proportionalitas* in the third and fourth books of his *Scriptum*.

It was only in *De veritate* that he explicitly called the analogy of God an *analogia proportionalitatis*, and then in contrast to pure metaphors about God.[78] In q. 2, a. 11, it was formally a question of giving a common *name*, and hence of the so-called "nominal analogy." This common predication is, however, based on a really existing relationship between the creature and God, and here the term *secundum analogiam* was still identified with *secundum proportionem*—the analogy was seen as a "convenientia secundum proportionem" (*loc. cit.*). This could, however, be of two kinds. There could be a "distantia *determinata*" between the two terms, so that the relationship was reciprocal.[79] This was a *proportio* in the strict sense of the word. There could, however, also be a relationship which was not a *proportio* (*determinata*), but a *similitudo proportionum* or *proportionalitas*. In *De veritate,* Thomas classified the analogy of God in this latter category, calling it a "similis habitudo aliquorum duorum ad alia duo"[80] or a "convenientia ... duorum ad invicem inter quae non sit proportio, sed magis similitudo duarum ad invicem proportionum."[81] Here, the double analogy is therefore the *analogia proportionis* and the *analogia proportionalitatis*. The examples

77 *In 3 Sent.* d. 1, q. 1, a. 1, ad 3 (p. 10).
78 See especially q. 2, a. 3, ad 4; a. 11, c. and ad 2, ad 4 and ad 6.
79 See also *Verit.* q. 2, a. 3, ad 4.
80 *Ibid.* q. 2, a. 3, ad 4.
81 *Ibid.* q. 2, a. 11.

given for the *analogia proportionis* are the same that were given for the *analogia duorum ad aliquid unum*. A measurable relationship, incorporating a *similitudo reciproca*, is required for this analogy—something that must be denied in the case of God. This to some extent raises the conjecture that the *proportionalitas* of *De veritate* is possibly only another name for the second kind of analogy, which was previously called an *analogia unius ad alterum*. The *proportionalitas* itself is subdivided here. First there is the symbolic proportionality or metaphor, in which the *similitudo proportionalitatis* is not to be found in the *significatio principalis*, so that there can really be a transference of *meaning*. This applies to those cases in which the creaturely mode enters the *significatum* itself of the perfections referred to. Second there is the non-symbolic proportionality, which applies to those cases in which the creaturely mode does not enter the *significatum* itself. In ad 4, Aquinas provided the following classification: "similitudo. . .ex eo quod *aliqua duo* participant unum" and "similitudo . . . ex eo quod *unum* habet habitudinem *determinatam* ad illud" and opposed these two to the "similitudo quae est secundum convenientiam proportionum." This third category was unknown in the first two books of the *Scriptum*, but what is equally interesting is that Thomas introduced a new shade of meaning, in *De veritate*, into the first two categories that had occurred so frequently in the first two books. What had previously been known as a "habitudo unius ad alterum" became here a "habitudo *determinata* unius ad alterum."[82] The *proportionalitas* thus became a superficially convenient term to express a "habitudo *infinita*." Thomas had recourse to the *proportionalitas* only because of the

[82] See also ad 6.

unmeasurable, inexpressible distance between God and creature—it is clear that his use of the *analogia proportionalitatis* is a denial on his part that there is any *measure common* to both God and creatures. It is clear that the *proportionalitas* is not used in the texts of *De veritate* in the sense of one single conceptual content applying in a proportional manner both to the Creator and to creatures. Thomas's temporary repudiation of the *analogia proportionis*, then, was occasioned by his wanting above all to affirm that no single creature had such a relationship with God that God's perfection could be *defined* from this relationship, because it was also in this context that he wrote: "nulla creatura habet *talem* habitudinem ad Deum per quam possit divina perfectio *determinari*" (*loc. cit.*, c. art.).

It is clear that Thomas preferred to give *proportio* its original, Euclidean meaning of measurable or proportional relationship in these questions of *De veritate*.[83] As far as I have been able to ascertain, he used the term *proportionalitas* in the context of the analogy of God for the first time in connection with the questions about the *Verbum incarnatum*,[84] in which the infinite distance between divine and human nature became a real difficulty in connection with the problem of the incarnation. It was precisely this difficulty which seems to have been the reason for Thomas's dropping the term *proportio*, with its implication of measurableness, in favour of the term *proportionalitas*, which, in the sphere of mathematics, wholly abstracted from the variants, and was thus able to take non-measurable relationships into account. But even then, Aquinas still remained conscious of the fact that *proportio* could also have a wider

---

83 See also *In 2 Sent.* d. 24, q. 3, a. 6, ad 3; *In Post. Analyt.* I, c. 5, lect. 12 (ed. Leon., n. 8).

84 *In 3 Sent.* d. 1, q. 1, a. 1, ad 3.

meaning, since he generally added an explicit reference to
this, even after giving priority to the term *proportionalitas*.[85]
This constant awareness was the reason why he returned
to his first formulations.

3. *De veritate* q. 23, a. 7, ad 9 is the text which shows
Aquinas's transition to the stage in which the term *proportionalitas* finally disappeared from his writings. He gave
two answers to the same objection that had been resolved
in earlier questions of these *Quaestiones disputatae* by the
proportionalitas, and he did this in such a way that the
proportionalitas was moved onto the second level. "Secundum quod proportio proprie in quantitatibus invenitur,
comprehendens duarum quantitatum ad invicem compara-
tarum *certam* mensuram," there is no *proportio* between
God and the creature, whereas, "secundum quod nomen
proportionis translatum est ad *quamlibet* habitudinem sig-
nificandam *unius rei ad rem aliam*," it is certainly permissible to speak of an "analogia proportionis unius ad alterum"
between the creature and God, "cum in aliqua habitudine
ipsum ad se habeat, utpote ab eo effectus et ei subiectus."[86]

85 See even as early as *In 4 Sent.* d. 49, q. 2, a. 1, ad 6; cf. *Potent.* q. 7,
a. 10, ad 9: "Si proportio intelligatur aliquis *determinatus* excessus, nulla
est Dei ad creaturam proportio. Si autem per proportionem intelligatur
habitudo sola, sic patet quod est inter Creatorem et creaturam."

86 *Loc. cit.* This distinction between *proportio stricte dicta* and *late dicta*
can be found everywhere in Thomas's work, although differently designated.
See *BT* q. 1, a. 2, ad 3; cf. *In 3 Sent.* d. 1, q. 1, a. 1, ad 3: "habitudo
duorum convenientium in eodem genere"—"habitudo duorum convenientium in eodem ordine"; *In 2 Sent.* d. 9, q. 1, a. 3, ad 5: "proportio secundum diversas species eiusdem generis"—"proportio secundum diversum
genus"; *In 2 Sent.* d. 30, q. 1, a. 1, ad 7: "proportio convenientium in
eadem natura"—"proportio potentiae ad actum"; *Verit.* q. 26, a. 1, ad 7:
"*determinata* habitudo quantitatis ad quantitatem"—"quaelibet habitudo";
I, q. 12, a. 1, ad 4: "*certa* habitudo unius quantitatis ad alterum"—"quaelibet

The *proportionalitas* is, however, valid as a second answer to the difficulty. It was introduced thus: "Vel potest dici, quod finiti ad infinitum, quamvis non possit esse proportio proprie accepta, tamen potest esse proportionalitas, quae est duorum proportionum similitudo . . .; et per hunc modum est similitudo inter creaturam et Deum, quia sicut se habet ad ea quae ei competunt, ita creatura ad sua propria."

When the texts in which Thomas had temporarily referred to the analogy of God as a *proportionalitas* are compared with those in which he discussed the *analogia proportionis unius ad alterum*, it becomes quite apparent that the *proportionalitas* materially covers the content of the *analogia proportionis*, that is, the "proportio creaturae ad Deum in quantum se habet ad ipsum ut effectus ad causam."[87] Thus, we have no more to learn about God from Thomas's *proportionalitas* than we had already learned from his *proportio*. This will become even clearer when the formal structure of his "nominal analogy" is examined more closely.

---

habitudo unius ad alterum"; *SCG* III, c. 54: "commensuratio proportione existente"—"quaecumque habitudo unius ad alterum"; *Potent.* q. 7, a. 10, ad 9; cf. *Quodl.* 10, q. 8, a. 1, ad 1: "determinatus excessus"—"habitudo sola" or "quaelibet habitudo"; *Verit.* q. 8, a. 1, ad 6: "habitudo quantitatis ad quantitatem"—"habitudo cuiuslibet ad rem alteram." A. Hayen has already drawn attention to this in his *L'intentionnel dans la philosophie de saint Thomas* (Museum Lessianum, sect. Phil., n. 25), Brussels and Paris 1942, 89–90.

87 I, q. 12, a. 1, ad 4. I am not making a critical study here of the idea of the *proportionalitas* in itself, but have merely aimed at providing an outline of Thomas's attitude towards the *proportionalitas*. The question as to whether the *proportionalitas* in itself can in fact have a metaphysical meaning is, however, quite different. For this question, see, for example, the controversy between E. L. Mascall, *Existence and Analogy*, London, New York and Toronto 1949, especially 108–109, and A. M. Farrer, *Finite and Infinite*, Westminster 1943, especially 52ff.

The Unity of "Nominal Analogy"

Aquinas first studied, in the first four articles of I, q. 13, the possibility of the divine names and the way in which they were used and based these names on the knowledge of God *ex creaturis*, with the result that creaturely elements necessarily entered into our knowledge and naming of God. He then proceeded to *compare* the *nomina creaturarum* with the *nomina divina* so as to be able to define more precisely what these names had in common, in other words, their similarity of name: hence the formulation of the problem of a. 5 in the prologue to I, q. 13, "Utrum nomina aliqua dicantur de Deo et creaturis univoce vel aequivoce." The problem is therefore purely grammatical, although it has a metaphysical basis.

He sets analogical predication over against univocity and equivocity. A name is said univocally of different subjects when its conceptual content and meaning, the *ratio nominis*, is common to two or more things. What we have here is an identical word-meaning, the *ratio* of which can be *predicated* equally of these subjects precisely because it is abstract and is not concerned with individual, concrete differences. The fact that it is univocally applicable to many things is therefore based on the abstract quality of its conceptual content. That is why the similarity of name between Creator and creature—"God is good," "the creature is good"—cannot be explained by the universality of the concept. Aquinas had, in any case, already pointed out in the preceding articles that we do not have such a single *ratio abstracta* embracing both God and the creature. We have no appropriate *ratio* of God, no *concept* of God—in our knowledge of God, we work with *rationes* or *definitiones* of creaturely perfections. And, even though we do find, in the creature, a "too much" that transcends the creaturely limits and objectively points to God, we cannot to such an extent disregard the creaturely mode in the concept, which is indissolubly connected with the creature, as to be left eventually with a real "concept of God." The similarity of name between God and the creature is therefore not based on the unity of the conceptual representation, as this can only be attributed to the creature and not to God. The identical name "goodness" thus does not cover an identical *ratio,* but, on the one hand, a *ratio* that is measured by the creaturely perfection and, on the other hand, a *"ratio" Dei* which is non-conceivable and which escapes us, but to which the creaturely content, by an inward dynamism, objectively refers.

On the other hand, however, there can be no question of equivocity. The similarity of name is equivocal when the same name pertains to different subjects in such a way that the content of meaning is quite different. This is a purely grammatical, linguistic phenomenon.

Thomas therefore concluded by calling the similarity of name between God and creature a similarity "secundum analogiam, idest proportionem." Nominal analogy always involves a *transference of name* from one subject to other subjects, just because these bear some relationship to this one subject and are for this reason called by the name of this first subject.[88]

It is a striking fact that Aquinas based the analogy of names on the reality, and not on the *ratio concepta* itself. A text from *Contra Gentiles* II, c. 16 seems to me to be fundamental to this question: "Quorumcumque *in rerum natura* est aliqua proportio et aliquis ordo, oportet *unum*

---

[88] P. Kreling has already referred to this meaning of "analogy" in Aquinas. See "De betekenis van de analogie in de kennis van God," *Verslag Veren. van Thom. Wijsbegeerte,* Nijmegen 1942, 31–54.

eorum esse ab alio vel *ambo ab aliquo uno.*"[89] It is precisely
these two cases which form the *basis* for a twofold analogical
predication, that is, the use of one name for two different
things, and this on the basis of an *analogia*. Aquinas therefore always distinguished two types of analogical predication,
according as to whether its basis was either a *proportio* (or
analogia) *unius ad alterum* or a *proportio duorum* (*vel
plurium*) *ad aliquid unum.*[90] This was expressed by Aquinas
in various ways: —*analogia proportionis duorum* (*vel plurium*) *ad unum*: "aliqua participant unum,"[91] "plura in uno"
or "multa in unum,"[92] "duorum ad tertium,"[93] "plurium
ad unum, scilicet finem, efficiens vel subiectum."[94]

—*analogia proportionis unius ad alterum*: "unum ab altero,"[95] "unum ad alterum,"[96] "unum imitatur aliud."[97]

A difficulty is presented by several texts in which there
is an apparent reference to a third type: "duo ad diversa"[98]
or "plurium ad plura subiecta."[99] Is this, then, an *analogia
plurium ad plura* or a *proportionalitas*? The examples mentioned are undoubtedly those of a proportionality. In *In 4
Metaphys., loc. cit.*, this analogy is contrasted with the *ana-*

[89] See also in *similitudo* terms, *Verit.* q. 2, a. 14; I, q. 65, a. 1, etc.
[90] See, for example, *In 1 Sent.* Prol., q. 1, a. 2, ad 2; *In 1 Sent.* d. 35,
q. 1, a. 4; *De princ. nat.* (ed. Text. Phil. Frib. 2, Fribourg and Louvain
1950, 102–104); *Verit.* q. 2, a. 11, ad 6; *BT* q. 1, a. 2, ad 3; *SCG* I, c. 34;
Potent. q. 7, a. 7; *In 4 Metaphys.* lect. 1; *In 5 Metaphys.* lect 8; *In 7
Metaphys.* lect. 4; *In 1 Ethic.* lect. 7; I, q. 13, a. 5; *Compend. Theol.* c.
27, etc.
[91] *In 1 Sent.* Prol., *loc. cit.*
[92] *In 1 Sent.* d. 35, *loc. cit.; SCG* I, c. 34; *In 5 Metaphys.* lect. 8; I, q.
13, a. 5; *Verit.* q. 2, a. 11, ad 6.
[93] *Potent.* q. 7, a. 7.
[94] *In 4 Metaphys.* lect. 1; *In 1 Ethic.* lect. 7; *De princ. nat., loc. cit.*
[95] *In 1 Sent.* Prol., *loc. cit.*
[96] *Verit.* q. 2, a. 11, ad 6; *SCG* I, c. 34; *Potent.* q. 7, a. 7; I, q. 13, a. 5.
[97] *In 1 Sent.* d. 35, *loc. cit., c.* and ad 6; *In 1 Sent.* Prol., *loc. cit.*
[98] *In 5 Metaphys.* lect. 8.
[99] *In 1 Ethic.* lect. 7.

logia plurium ad unum, and the example mentioned points
to a metaphorical proportionality. In the second text quoted,
this is less clear. But we may safely conclude that the *analogia plurium ad plura* is only a form of the *analogia unius
ad alterum*, and that for Thomas, in the few texts in which,
under the influence of Aristotle, he refers to *proportionalitas*, this is based on the *proportio* and not *vice versa*, that
is, the *proportio* being based on the *proportionalitas*.

From the point of view of textual criticism, then, we
have to adhere to the two types—*unius ad alterum* and *duorum (plurium) ad unum*. Basically, both these types go
back to the *same* analogy-structure, *proportio ad unum
aliquid* or, as Thomas himself formulated it, "analoga *quia*
proportionantur ad unum,"[100] "dicuntur secundum analogiam, *id est* secundum proportionem ad unum."[101] Now this
real *unum aliquid* may pertain to the so-called *analogata*
themselves, in which case it is a question of a *proportio
unius ad alterum*, or it may not pertain to these, in which
case it is a question of an *analogia duorum (plurium) ad
aliquid unum (tertium)*. The last type is based on the first,
which is the fundamental type. This emerges clearly from
the repeated example of both analogies—*ens* is said analogically as the name of *qualitas* and *quantitas*. *Qualitas* and *quantitas* here are the *analogata*, whereas the concrete *substantia*
is the point of reference or the *analogans*—*ens* is the proper
name only of the substance. This is the *analogia duorum
ad unum* term, but because one of the things called *ens*
is the proper *ens* and communicates its name to the other.
The primary term is therefore rather the *analogans* and,
properly speaking, not an *analogatum*. It is clear from this
that the *analogia unius ad alterum* is the basis of the *analogia
duorum ad tertium*—because separately *qualitas* and *quan-

100 *In 11 Metaphys.* lect. 3.
101 *Compend. Theol.* c. 27.

titas have a *proportio* to the substance (thus, because of the *unum ad alterum*), both bear a mutual relationship towards each other, but *per respectum ad substantium*. In the *analogia duorum ad tertium*, the mutual *similitudo* of the *analogata* is therefore reciprocal, while this does not, in itself, need to be so in the case of the *analogia unius ad alterum*.

It is important to note that the *unum aliquid* with which we are always concerned here is not a *ratio abstracta communis*. The *unum* to which something (or more things) is directed is referred to as a "causa efficiens,"[102] a "causa finalis,"[103] a "causa exemplaris,"[104] or a "subiectum."[105] What we have here is not a conceptual unity, a *ratio communis abstracta*, but an "unum numero."[106] The things are in a definite relationship to a real something which, *because of this relationship*, communicates its name to the subjects concerned. As a result, analogy always includes a *secundum prius et posterius*. *Analogice* and *secundum prius et posterius* are identical—"analogice, *idest* secundum prius et posterius."[107] The *name* that is attributed *secundum prius* to the central reality is also ascribed to or used for the realities that are dependent on the central reality. That,

---

102 *In 1 Sent.* Prol., *loc. cit.; De princ. nat., loc. cit.; In 4 Metaphys., loc. cit.; In 1 Ethic., loc. cit.*

103 *De princ. nat., loc. cit.; In 4 Metaphys., loc. cit.; In 1 Ethic., loc. cit.*
104 *In 1 Sent.* d. 35, *loc. cit.*

105 *In 1 Sent.* d. 35, *loc. cit.; De princ. nat., loc. cit.; In 4 Metaphys., loc. cit.; In 1 Ethic., loc. cit.*

106 *In 4 Metaphys.* lect. 1 (ed. Marietti 1950, n. 536).

107 I, q. 5, a. 6, ad 3; *De malo*, q. 7, a. 1, ad 1; I–II, q. 61, a. 1, ad 1: I–II, q. 88, a. 8, ad 1; II–II, q. 120, a. 2, etc. The difficulty presented by *Verit.* q. 2, a. 11, ob. 6 and ad 6 can be resolved from the definite standpoint that Thomas provisionally took up there; anyway, we can regard something in itself and thus "define" it, but in this case the definition is incomplete. But if we define it as geared to the whole and as dependent on God, then God really enters the definition of every finite being. See the interpretation of this text in Francis Sylvester, *In Contra Gentiles*, I, c. 34.

then, is the basis of analogical predication. It is therefore quite outside the *ratio formalis* of analogy, whether the *ratio nominis*, that is, the conceptual content (of the central reality), is or is not really to be found in the realities referred to. It is true that this is of great importance for the noetic structure of our knowledge of God, but it is not important for the problem of analogical predication, with the result that both the metaphors of God and the divine attributes proper show, in their function as "analogical predicates," the same structure *proper to analogy.* Whether or not the *una forma* that is encountered in the real so-called primary *analogon* is inherent to the other subjects is a question that is outside the *ratio formalis analogiae.* For this reason, Thomas gives examples of the analogy as a *proportio ad unum*, in which the *forma* of the *analogans was* inherent in the so-called *analogata,*[108] as well as examples of purely extrinsic attribution.[109] Analogy is therefore essentially an *attributio*, no matter whether the *una forma* is or is not inherent in the different subjects. Thomas thus always spoke of *"attribuere* nomen unius alteri," even if the said perfection was realised, deficiently perhaps but inwardly, in the *subjectum attributionis.*[110] Analogical predications of God therefore mean, in *linea analogiae*, simply that we transfer the *name* of the one to the other because of the real relationship of the creatures to God. Thomas did not say that the *ratio concepta* is attributed to God. What he did say is that the *name* is attributed to him and that we *tend towards* and designate God via the *ratio* that is directly covered by the name (the *ratio nominis*). This,

---

108 See, for example, *In 4 Metaphys.* lect. 1 (n. 535); *substantia* and *accidens* are both really *ens,* although the *accidens* is *ens* only in relation to the substance.

109 See, for example, I, q. 13, a. 5: *sanum* is said of *animal* and of *medicina.*

110 See, for example, *Potent.* q. 3, a. 5, *Compend theol.* c. 27.

then, is what Thomas meant by analogical knowledge of
God. "Ex eo enim quod alias res comparamus ad Deum
sicut ad suam primam originem, huiusmodi *nomina,* quae
significant perfectiones aliarum rerum, Deo *attribuimus.*"[111]
The *attributio* refers formally to the transference of the
name. There is no reference at all here to an "analogical
concept" predicated in a proportionally unified manner of
different subjects. The *universale proportionale* has no place
in Thomas's view. For him the analogy was not to be found
in concepts. For analogical predication or naming in connection with God was used by Thomas precisely in order to
be able, to some extent, to express a certain real identity
that cannot be conceptually grasped either specifically or
even generically.

The content of the analogical predication is, in super-
ficial cases of analogy, a definite conceptual content which
is, as such, said univocally of a definite reality (the so-called
central reality—for example, *sanum* as a term with the
conceptual content *sanitas animalis*). The other realities
which, taken in the concrete, have a relationship to this
sanitas animalis each have their own *definitio.* As such, however, they are not formally regarded as analogical. They are
only regarded as analogical when their relationship to the
sanitas animalis is kept in mind. In that case, they are,
analogously, themselves called "healthy," that is to say, the
one concrete health of the biological being enters in its
concrete definite quality into the definition of the other
subjects that are, in one way or another, related to it. There
is, therefore, no question here of *one abstract concept*
that in a confused but actual manner includes the differences of the subject. *"Alia* et *alia* est significatio nominis,
sed *una illarum significationum* clauditur *in significationibus*

111 *Compend. theol.* c. 27.

aliis. Unde manifestum est quod analogice dicuntur"[112]— "*eadem* est enim sanitas quam animal suscipit, urina significat, medicina facit et diaeta conservat."[113] The *prius*-reality, the name of which we transfer to the other subjects, thus enters into the definition itself of the other subjects.[114]

In his commentary on Aristotle's *Metaphysics*, Thomas does, it is true, have a text that has been turned by many scholars to account in favour of the *universale proportionale*—"Aliquid praedicatur de diversis . . . , quandoque secundum *rationes* quae *partim sunt diversae* et *partim non diversae.*"[115] This should, however, be understood in its context—the diversity is there "secundum quod important diversas habitudines ad aliquid unum," the unity, on the other hand, "secundum quod istae diversae habitudines referentur ad *unum* aliquid." This *unum* is an "unum numero,"[116] and thus a concrete reality—one *ratio, univocally* applicable to one concrete reality. The diverse *analogata*, and therefore their "diversae rationes," on the other hand, express a relationship to this "una ratio" of the concrete *analogans.* Thus, "ratione diversa referuntur ad unum, sicut est in analogicis."[117] This is Aquinas's usual thesis—the *proportio ad unum* is the basis for a transferenece of name *secundum prius et posterius.*

This *prius et posterius* includes the entire network that exists in a more or less intimate manner between things or that we ourselves introduce, because of bases in reality,

---

112 I, q. 13, a. 10.

113 *In 4 Metaphys.* lect. 1 (n. 537).

114 See, for example, I, q. 16, a. 6; I–II, q. 20, a. 3, ad 3; III, q. 60, a. 1, ad 3; I, q. 13, a. 6; SCG II, 15; cf. I, q. 76, a. 4, arg. 3; II–II, q. 26, a. 1; SCG I, c. 32, etc.

115 *In 4 Metaphys.* lect. 1 (n. 535) and *In 11 Metaphys.* lect. 3 (n. 2197): "ratio partim diversa partim una."

116 *In 4 Metaphys.* lect. 1 (n. 536).

117 *Ibid.* (n. 568).

between things themselves. It is in this light that we should interpret the threefold division of analogy given by Thomas in *In 1 Sent.* d. 19, q. 5, a. 2, ad 1, where he refers to an analogy "secundum intentionem tantum," "secundum esse et secundum intentionem" and finally "secundum esse et non secundum intentionem." This passage is not concerned with a division of the analogical predication, but with the nature of the real or non-real *proportio* between things, on which the analogical predication is based.[118]

---

[118] Aquinas's division of analogy referred to above is perfectly reconcilable with the following division of the basis of analogy:

A. *Analogia duorum (vel plurium) ad unum tertium*

   a. "Secundum intentionem tantum"; example: *sanum* is said analogically of *medicina* and *urina* with regard to *sanitas animalis* (see, for example, I, q. 13, a. 5; I, q. 16, a. 6; I–II, q. 20, a. 3, ad 3; *In 4 Metaphys.* lect. 1, n. 535; *In 5 Metaphys.* lect. 8, n. 879; *SCG* I, c. 34). This analogical transference of name is therefore founded on relationships that we ourselves situate in reality, on a basis of a real foundation. *Sanum* as such is, however, an *univocum*.

   b. "Secundum intentionem et esse"; example: *ens* is said of *qualitas* and *quantitas* with regard to *substantia* (see, for example, *Potent.* q. 7, a. 7; *Verit.* q. 2, a. 11, ad 6). Here, the *content* of what is said is real (*secundum esse*) in both *analogata*, but it is real in that it is dependent on the being of the substance, which is the proper *unum*. It is also characteristic of Thomas that he never calls the *analogy of being* a *proportionalitas*. The examples of the so-called analogy of being are in his case always substance as opposed to the accidents or the creatures as opposed to God. "Omnia alia praedicamenta habent rationem entis a substantia; ideo modus entitatis substantiae, scilicet esse quid, participatur secundum similitudinem *proportionis* in omnibus aliis praedicamentis" (*In 7 Metaphys.* lect. 7, n. 1334). The *substantia* itself is a participation of God: "hoc ipso quod creatura habet substantiam modificatam et finitam, demonstrat quod sit a primo principio" (I, q. 9, a. 6). The analogy of being in the Cajetanian sense would appear to be unknown to Aquinas. It is, however, outside the scope of this chapter to examine in greater detail the problem of the Thomist *ens commune* with regard to God as the *principium entis*.

B. *Analogia unius ad alterum*

   a. "Secundum intentionem tantum": *sanum* said of *animal* and of *medicina* (I, q. 13, a. 5; *Verit.* q. 2, a. 11; q. 21, a. 4, ad 2).

   b. "Secundum intentionem et esse": *ens* said of *substantia* and *acci-*

If we now apply this formal structure of analogy to our
so-called names of God, we shall come to the following insights. In view of the fact that the *secundum prius et posterius* is essential to every analogical predication, Thomas,
after having established the analogical character of our
names of God (I, q. 13, a. 5), as a matter of course asked the
question: "supposito quod dicantur analogice, utrum dicantur de Deo prius vel de creaturis."[119]

"In analogicis oportet quod nomen secundum unam significationem acceptum ponatur in definitione eiusdem nominis secundum alias significationes accepti."[120] This is important if we are, by way of the theory of analogy, to find
confirmation for Thomas's idea concerning the non-conceptual intellectual dimension in our knowledge of God.

This is a simple matter in the case of the so-called metaphorical names of God, where it is clear that the creature is
the *prius* or the central reality from which the creaturely
names are predicated analogically of God. The proper names
of God, however, pose a more difficult problem. It was
clear from I, q. 13, a. 1 to a. 4 that what is indicated by
such names is essentially present in God—God is good. But,
in this context, Thomas at once makes the distinction that
was traditional at the time between the *res significata* and

dens; wisdom said of God and of man (*Potent.* q. 7, a. 7; *SCG* I, c. 34;
De malo q. 7, a. 1, etc.).

The "secundum esse et non secundum intentionem" refers in Thomas's
work to the so-called perfections which are univocal for the logician and
analogical for the metaphysician—corporeality is said univocally of the sub-
lunar bodies and the celestial bodies, but the *esse* of corporeality—that is,
their concrete state of being physical—is completely different in the *corpora
corruptibilia* and the medieval *corpora incorruptibilia caelestia* (*In 1 Sent.*
d. 19, q. 5, a. 2, ad 1; see *Potent.* q. 7, a. 7, ad I in contrar.). "Corporeality"
does become a *ratio communis* if we take a purely abstract standpoint.

[119] The title of I, q. 13, a. 6, according to the prologue to q. 13.
[120] I, q. 13, a. 10.

the *impositio nominis,* to which, as I have said, the *ratio nominis* has still to be added. Ontologically, the names that point to transcendental perfections are attributed, *per prius,* to God—God is, simply and of his very nature, good, while the creature is only good as participating in God's goodness. The creature is God's goodness itself, *as participated.* God, as ontologically *prius,* thus enters into the very definition of the creature. Nonetheless, we *know* God only via his manifestation in the creature, with the result that it is in and through our knowledge of the goodness of the creature that we reach and name the goodness of God. In this way, the creature is the central reality of all our analogical names of God. And since our idea of God's goodness remains, as we have seen, a creaturely idea, we are bound to say that, in our knowledge and naming of God, the creaturely idea of goodness enters into the defining naming of God's goodness. In other words, for our knowledge of God, the creaturely concept always remains the *prius* from which we can objectively only aim at and mean the ontological *prius,* without however ever conceptually grasping and understanding God. Analogy is a manner of *predication* and it moves therefore on the level of the *impositio nominis.* That is why, for our *explicit* knowledge, the creaturely reality is always the *prius* to which we have to refer in order to know anything about God. If we mean the implicit content, then the name "goodness" applies primarily to God. If, however, we mean the explicit conceptual contents, then these apply primarily to the creature, but it should be understood that—because of the implicit, real content—an objective view is opened onto what God really is. "Respondeo et dico quod nomen alicuius rei nominatae a nobis dupliciter potest accipi: quia vel est expressivum aut significativum conceptus intellectus, . . . et sic nomen prius est in creaturis quam in Deo. Aut inquantum est manifestativum quiddita-

tis rei nominatae exterius, et sic est prius in Deo."[121] As
far as the *conceptual* element in our knowledge of God is
concerned, we work inevitably and always with creaturely
concepts—we have no concept of God. That our knowledge
of God is capable of grasping reality cannot be derived from
the conceptual element in itself and *as such*. Thomas never
regarded God and the creature (in his non-essentialist statements) as *inferiora* of a general concept *ens commune*. The
being of the creatures themselves is a *participatio esse divini:*
"unumquodque participat esse *secundum habitudinem*
quam habet ad primum essendi principium."[122] For
Thomas, the analogy of being was a *proportio immediata
unius* (that is, of the creature) *ad alterum* (that is, to God)
with, as an inward consequence, the real ordering of the
being of the created beings to the *esse subsistens*. "Creatura
enim non habet esse nisi secundum quod a primo ente descendit (objective, real *analogia* or participation) nec *nomi-
natur* ens nisi in quantum ens primum imitatur (nominal
analogy because of the objective *proportio*.)"[123] It is clear
from *Contra Gentiles* I, c. 33, that Aquinas speaks only of a
"communitas nominis" ("non *rationis*") and that he does
so because of a relationship of participation: "Consideratur
enim in huiusmodi nominum communitate, ordo causae et
causati." If we continue to use the term "analogy," we must
say that all our affirmations concerning God are analogical,
because we know God only *from the creature*—because, in
other words, the creature *shows* God to us in the direct extension of (but also within) the *transcendentalia*. The basis
of the reality of our knowledge of God is therefore neither

---

121 *In Ep. ad Ephes.* c. 3, lect. 4 (ed. Marietti 1953, 43, n. 169).

122 *In lib. de causis* c. 25 (ed. Text. Phil. Frib. 4/5, Fribourg 1945, 126);
see *De substantiis separatis* c. 8; *In 2 Metaphys.* lect. 2, n. 290–296; *SCG* II,
c. 15; *Potent.* q. 7, a. 7, ad 2; *Quodl.* 12, q. 5, a. 1; *In 1 Sent.* d. 43, q.
1, a. 2, ad 4.

123 *In 1 Sent.* Prol., q. 1, a. 2, ad 2.

a so-called proportionally one, proper *concept,* nor the subjective dynamism of the spirit, which makes the concept into a projection of God, but rather the *objective* dynamism of the content of being (that is, the so-called *transcendentalia*) to which man's spirit fully consents in an act of intellectual tending or projection. This seems to me to express most precisely Thomas's most intimate thought concerning our knowledge of God. I call it Thomas's most intimate thought, since texts can be found in Thomas's writing, even in his later works, in which, under the influence of Avicenna, unmistakably essentialist echoes are discernible. It is, however, at the same time necessary to point out that Thomas did not analyse any further the structure of the knowledge of this distinction between the transcendental perfections and the predicamental conceptual contents. He merely affirmed what is meaningful in this distinction and denied that we have any authentic concepts of God, that is, that we may *grasp* God purely in notions. The consequences of this loyal affirmation of the transcendental character of the content of being for the noetic structure itself of the objective act of knowing were not subjected by Thomas to further analysis. His entire synthesis, however, shows clearly that he seriously meant what he was saying when he wrote "in intellectu humano puritas intellectualis cognitionis non penitus obscuratur."[124] In other words, human knowledge is borne up by the veiled, non-conceptual dimension of knowing.

---

124 *Verit.* q. 13, a. 3. As is shown by the context, *intellectualis* is contrasted with *rationalis.*

Table of Original Publications

INDEX